Traditions of
Trinity and Leith

D1634974

On more than one occasion the fortunes of Leith have been the point on which the whole history of our country has turned.

John Russell, *The Story of Leith*

When Provost Drummond built the North Bridge in 1769, he contemplated that it should become an access to Leith, as well as to the projected New Town. Indeed, he seems to have been obliged to make it pass altogether under that semblance, in order to conciliate the people: for upon the plate sunk under the foundations of the bridge, it is soley described as the opening of a road to Leith.

Robert Chambers, *Traditions of Edinburgh*

In the beginning of the present [nineteenth] century, and before the roads to Queensferry and Granton were constructed, the chief or only one in this quarter was that which, between hedgerows and trees, led to Trinity . . .

James Grant, *Old and New Edinburgh*

Traditions of Trinity and Leith

JOYCE M. WALLACE

Foreword by
PETER ROBINSON
Vice-President
Edinburgh Architectural Association

Illustrations
from photographs
by the Author

JOHN DONALD PUBLISHERS LTD.
EDINBURGH

To my Mother
who grew up in Trinity

ISBN 0 85976 124 X

Filmset by H.M. Repros, Glasgow
and printed in Great Britain by Bell & Bain Ltd., Glasgow.

Foreword

IN a different world Edinburgh might well have been a distant suburb of the City of Leith and not the other way around. For nature had blessed that part of the shore of the Forth with all the advantages of a safe haven and a flat site. It was something that the burgesses of Edinburgh well understood in a more robust age of merchant intrigue. Perched high up on a hill, two miles from the sea, they had long seen Leith and the shore as a threat to their livelihoods. Their very survival depended on controlling the port and the people, and it was a struggle where power and prestige prevailed.

Almost ninety years of independence from Edinburgh from 1833 to 1920 stamped a mark of individuality on Trinity and Leith that has survived Luftwaffe bombs and the more sustained and effective ravages of decay. Officialdom may have banished Leithers to Sighthill and beyond, but their hearts are still by the sea. Refugees return to shop and to reminisce, although happily now more are coming back to work. The Leith Project, not long under way, has already made an impact on the Town so that a certain self-confidence is returning to areas blighted by changing trade patterns and more than half a century of neglect. Suddenly there is a future, and the natural advantages of the site and a sturdy independent spirit may yet succeed.

Leith is above all a port of rich contrast and unlikely associations, and Trinity is its western suburb. Together they have looked out to the world. They have weathered tyrants and storms, sieges and plague — surprisingly the last case was reported as recently as 1905 — and they have sheltered great international figures, like Hans Christian Andersen and Robert Louis Stevenson — born in Inverleith — as well as ships. Neither was there any shortage of local characters, such as the cadaverous and asthmatic Hugo Arnot and the notorious Green Jenny who haunted the unwary in the night haar. There was nothing dull about Trinity and Leith past.

This is a story that is unashamedly about the past and it is as much about places as people. Joyce Wallace is an accomplished amateur historian whose family associations with Trinity and Leith go back more than a century. For many years she has patiently researched and recorded the area from original material and developed an understanding which brings to life Edinburgh's northern shoreline and immediate hinterland. It is a unique and lively record, conveniently gathering material on Trinity, in particular, for the first time.

This is a book where you can smell the sea salt and watch the trams shuggle in and out of Shrubhill. Joyce Wallace has touched the weeping walls of Bangholm Bower and you can feel the blood red ochre.

Peter Robinson
Edinburgh Architectural Association

Acknowledgements

GRATEFUL acknowledgement is made to Dr W. S. Robertson and Dr P. Barron, whose knowldge of Trinity has been of great assistance in the writing of this book, to the Royal Incorporation of Architects in Scotland who arranged for the reading of the text by Mr Peter Robinson, Vice-President of the Edinburgh Architectural Association, and to the staff of the Edinburgh Room of the Edinburgh Public Library.

Contents

CHAPTER 1

Inverleith

BEFORE the New Town of Edinburgh was conceived in progressive civic minds within the cabined, cribbed Old Town in the late eighteenth century, the City, perched high and narrow on its long volcanic ridge, was flanked on the immediate north by the valley of the Nor' Loch and on the immediate south by the valley of the little River Tumble which had been domesticated into the lower residential thoroughfare parallel to the High Street known as the Cowgate. The wider environment of this rockbound, urban island consisted of rough, open country with scattered farms and hamlets, surrounded on all sides by bogland or muirland and an occasional loch and hill. Marshes, dangerous after nightfall to the unwary traveller, lay to the west, stretching out towards Corstorphine village where a lamp was hung in the gable of the Parish Church as a guide to wayfarers before the ground was drained and laid out with roads. To the south lay the Borough Loch, later to be replaced by the green, tree-planted hollow known as The Meadows, and the Borough Muir on which the ancient oaks, that had supplied the timber, or 'timmer', frontages of the High Street houses since the time of James IV, were destined to come down and the residential streets of Marchmont and The Grange (the old Grange of St. Giles having been situated on the moor) to go up during the course of the nineteenth century. To the east was the sea with its seaport and then, further round the coast, the Figgate Muir, later to be subdued into the popular Victorian bathing resort of Portobello. And on the north, windswept and salt-sprayed from the Firth of Forth, the lands of Wardie spread out their tough and uncompromising old Muir at the foot of the long, exposed hillside that bottomed out in the valley of the Forth, with the Kingdom of Fife across the water.

1

At a remote period Inverleith was the name given to a very wide stretch of terrain round the mouth of the Water of Leith river and, as John Russell has pointed out in *The Story of Leith*, the shortened form of Leith was soon adopted by the thriving town which grew from the tiny village then occupying the site now known as The Shore, an area which, as the discovery of skulls, stone hammers and bronze axes testifies, probably witnessed human settlement at an earlier date than Edinburgh. Inverleith — the longer form — was then confined to the lands lying further up the river, and this usage has remained to the present day.

James Grant, the late nineteenth-century historian of Edinburgh, describes the appearance of Wardie Muir, first in its original, virgin state and then after its suburban transformation which took place largely in the early decades of last century: 'Wardie Muir must once have been a wide, open and desolate space extending from Inverleith and Warriston to the shore of the Firth; and from North Inverleith Mains, of old called Blaw Wearie, on the west, to Bonnington on the east . . . Now it is intersected by streets and roads studded with fine villas rich in gardens and teeming with fertility'. But Inverleith itself was sometimes called Innerleith (Inner-lyth on Blaeu's atlas of 1654), and the probability that the Water from which it takes its name was a more substantial river in the past than it is now is borne out by a history of periodic flooding in the earlier centuries. The deliberate redirection of springs feeding the river is probably the main cause of its diminution. The prefix 'Inver' (an alternative form of 'Aber') from the Gaelic 'Inbhir' means a place where sea and river meet, and thus indicates a much deeper and larger estuary with the possibility that the Leith was navigable as far inland as Inverleith or perhaps even Stockbridge. It was in fact at one time known as 'the Great River of the Water of Leith'. In 1659 there were 'unheard of tempests, storms and inundations of water whilk destroyed . . . eleven mills . . . upon the Water of Leith'. In 1794 there was a dangerous 'spate in the river', and in 1821 'a coachman with his horse was

Fig. 1. Inverleith House in the Royal Botanic Garden. An 18th century building which was once the home of the Rocheids of Inverleith.

carried down the stream and drowned near the gate of Inverleith'.

The baronial estate of Inverleith is of ancient origin, having been mentioned in the Charters of Robert the Bruce. In the fifteenth century it came into the possession of the Touris — or Towers — family, and two hundred years later into that of the strangely named Rocheids, an appellation said to have originated in a physical peculiarity of a member of that family. Sir James Rocheid, who acquired the lands in 1678, had been suspected, while Town Clerk of Edinburgh, of embezzlement but appears successfully to have survived both this and other stigmas. Another James, the last representative of that line, lived in Inverleith House, built by him in the heart of what is now the Royal Botanic Garden in 1773, and into which he and his mother, Mrs Rocheid of Inverleith, moved when it had become necessary to abandon the earlier and deteriorated house on an adjoining site. Even for those days when extreme formality was more honoured in the acceptance than the breach, they stood on ceremony to such an extent that Lord Cockburn thought it worth recording in his *Memorials*. Grant called him 'a man of inordinate vanity and family pride', and Cockburn, with relish and perhaps a hint of nostalgia, recalled the ostentatious style in which his mother drove out in her mulberry-coloured coach, where she sat 'like a Nautilus in its shell', down the drive which more public-spirited times have pedestrianised into Arboretum Avenue, past the lodge and the gate-piers surmounted by their ancient and curious stone lions said to have come originally from Edinburgh Castle, over the Stock Bridge and so to town, stared after by a local populace suitably awed by her magnificence. On entering an assembly 'she would sail like a ship from Tarshish, gorgeous in velvet or rustling silk' and 'take possession of the centre of a large sofa', covering it 'with her bravery, the graceful folds seeming to lay themselves over it like summer waves'. She presided in similar pomp over her son's dinners 'to the very last day almost of a prolonged life'. The lodge, the gate-piers and the lions still identify the old entrance, though their association with Inverleith House now tends to be forgotten.

In 1863 the house and its immediate policies became the domain of the Scots historian and antiquary Cosmo Lang, who claimed he could trace the lands of Inverleith back to their possession by the baker of King William the Lion. Fourteen acres of the Rocheid estate had in 1820 become the permanent location of the Botanic Garden, a garden which had first been planted as long ago as 1670 at Holyrood, where it was known as the Physic Garden, and then transferred in 1763 to another site near Haddington Place in Leith Walk. After the death of Cosmo Lang in 1874 Inverleith House and the surrounding land were bought by the City and added, as an extension, to the Garden where the house provided a finely situated residence for the Keeper. Its adaptation as the National Gallery of Modern Art was carried out in 1960 but the Gallery has now removed to the former John Watson's School at Belford.

In St. Bernard's Row, immediately opposite the lodge and gate-piers, the house formerly known as Malta Green has recently been restored. Built about 1840, such external features as a label moulding on the main frontage and miniature battlementing on the roof have lent credence to the description of its architectural style as English Tudor.

The attractive, late Georgian houses in Inverleith Row, described by Grant as 'handsome villas and other good residences', were planned by Thomas Brown and, starting in 1823, were built on ground which had belonged to the 'eminent agriculturist', James Rocheid. The only surviving reference to his name within the bounds of his inheritance is the little Rocheid Path which runs by the Water of Leith between Arboretum Road and Canonmills. The ancient village of Canonmills lay within the Barony of Broughton and owed its origin 'to the same source as the Burgh of Canongate, having been founded by the Augustine Canons of Holyrood'. Here David I built a corn mill for the canons, and also for the use of the local inhabitants, on the south side of the Water of Leith, which was driven by a lade diverted from it. To this mill the Incorporation of Bakers in the Canongate were 'thirled', being bound either to grind their corn there or to pay a fine. Canonmills House at a later date, and Canonmills Loch with its wildfowl, lay further to the south, the house being superseded by Eyre Crescent, with its church, in 1881.

Haig's Distillery was a well-known feature at Canonmills towards the end of the eighteenth century, and it was there that one of the 'meal mob' riots took place in 1783. A report was circulating that potatoes and oats were being used for distilling purposes while, in that year of food scarcity and high prices, the people were being left to starve. The Riot Act was read, firearms were issued for defence to the Haig employees, and the buildings were saved from destruction, though one of the rioters was killed. The disturbances lasted for several days and plans were made to mobilise the servants of country houses in the vicinity of Edinburgh, if required, to put down the disorders.

The original Canonmills bridge, consisting of a single arch, was built in 1761 and was of considerable importance as it provided convenient access to Inverleith and Trinity for wheeled traffic, and horse-drawn carriages were soon crossing it on their way to the new country residences that were now being built — small, unpretentious houses for the most part and intended only for summer occupation. It was replaced in 1840 by a bridge carried over the river (which can still run high and brown with floodwater from its source above Harperrigg Reservoir, into and then out of which manmade sheet of water it flows, after winter snows) on three arches. This later bridge was widened in 1896. To the east, at Warriston Road, the goods railway line to Ferry Road is carried over the street and the stream by a substantial stone bridge constructed in 1841.

Between the two bridges an eighteenth-century, whitewashed, pantile-roofed farm cottage has somehow managed to survive in Warriston Road. As it is a farm cottage as opposed to a farm house, it may be supposed that the farm was very small as well with, possibly, a cow, a goat and a few pigs, and it is not difficult to imagine hens strutting and scratching in the little garden which lay in front of the entrance on the other side, away from the road and the river. In the following century it became the gatehouse of Heriothill Station and after that the home of a 'mussel boiler' who left it littered with shells. After more recent rescue from dereliction, it had the good fortune to be transformed into the Canonmills Pottery and a kiln chimney was attached to its further gable. The pottery, an ideal use for the building, has however been closed as the whole site, which is bounded on the south by

Fig. 2. An 18th century farm cottage that has survived modern housebuilding in Warriston Road.

Broughton Road, was acquired for building development in 1982, and the garden ground which had been restored and replanted as a typical old cottage garden by the potter has been destroyed. The cottage itself, being the subject of a preservation order, stands a fighting chance of being permitted to remain, but the rural charm and character of the Canonmills section of Warriston Road has now disappeared, and the little cottage can only survive, at best, deprived of its complementary environment.

Also at Canonmills, on the north bank of the Leith, is all that remains of what Grant calls 'the peculiar edifice known as Tanfield Hall'. It was 'an extensive suite of buildings designed, it has been said, to represent a Moorish fortress, and was erected in 1825 as oil-gas works, but speedily turned to other purposes'. It is principally remembered today as the place in which the first General Assembly of the Free Church of Scotland was held in 1843 when the Disruption brought well over four hundred protesters against the injustices of patronage out of St. Andrew's Church in George Street and onto 'the long steep street' that led towards Tanfield Hall where they proceeded to elect Dr Thomas Chalmers as their first Moderator. The name of Tanfield is taken from a former tanyard at this point on the river bank and the buildings here were for many years the printing works of Messrs Morrison and Gibb.

No. 8 Inverleith Row, an imposing Classical house restored by Ian G. Lindsay & Partners a few years ago, beside the eastern entrance to the Botanic Gardens, was designed by W.H. Playfair, the architect of the Royal Scottish Academy in Princes Street, who, in 1818, was optimistically appointed architect for a projected New Town between Edinburgh and Leith. The imposing terraces around the Calton Hill and the elegantly classical Windsor Street were built, as well as Hillside Crescent and Leopold Place, but the scheme to extend Edinburgh's Georgian development from Calton to Leith Links was much too grandiose and costly ever to be a practical proposition.

In recent times, Sir Thomas Innes of Learney, the late Lord Lyon King-of-Arms, lived for many years in Inverleith Row at No. 35, as did the Edinburgh historian and writer, the late Moray McLaren and his actress wife, Lennox Milne, at No. 29. The well-known Edinburgh Jewellers, Messrs Hamilton and Inches, lived here also, the Hamiltons at No. 17 (which is now an Abbeyfield House for the elderly) and the Inches at No. 18.

At No. 8 Howard Place (a row of front-gardened villas built in 1809), on the opposite side of the street and closer to Canonmills, was born, in 1850, the only child of his parents, the delicate boy who was to become known to the world by three initials, R.L.S. In 1853 the Stevenson family removed to 1 Inverleith Terrace, which was just across the road and which had previously been occupied by William Edmonstoune Aytoun, Professor of Rhetoric at Edinburgh University and famous contributor to *Blackwood's Magazine*, and his wife Jane, daughter of Professor John Wilson, better known to readers of that illustrious publication as Christopher North. Both houses proved to be in too damp a locality for the health of Robert Louis and his mother, from whom he had inherited the weak condition of his chest, and in 1857 the family left low-lying Inverleith for the windier but drier Heriot Row in the New Town up the hill.

At the foot of the slope leading down from Broughton Road to Canonmills a bronze plaque on the wall of a building at the corner of Munro Place records the often overlooked fact that it contains the Hall in which, about 1857, Stevenson first went to school. Above the inscription is a head of the poet in relief. At the top of the hill the Royal Navy and Royal Marine Club occupies the nineteenth-century Heriot Hill House at its junction with Broughton Road.

At the north end of Inverleith Row, near Goldenacre, No. 52 was for many years the home of a historically interesting old army officer, Lieutenant-General William Crockat, whose name, says James Grant, 'was associated with the exile and death of Napoleon in St. Helena'. In 1807 he was 'gazetted an ensign in the 20th Regiment of Foot' and saw distinguished service in Spain in the famous battles of Vimiera, Corunna and Vittoria. At the end of the French wars he went with his regiment to the now legendary island of captivity where he became the last officer to be given charge of the 'caged eagle of St. Helena' who died there under his guardianship. The then Captain Crockat was sent home with dispatches to announce the news. After these historic events he spent the rest of his active life in India, retiring in 1830 to Edinburgh where, 'in spite of war, wounds and fever', he lived for nearly half a century before he passed away, in 1874, at a green old age, in his villa at Inverleith Row, 'a hale old relic of other times'.

Close at hand, near the junction with Ferry Road, stands St. James Episcopal Church, built in the middle Gothic style in 1888 by Sir Rowand Anderson. This spacious church has a good and interesting interior, the chancel walls being painted in fresco with representations of saints and martyrs by William Hole, R.S.A., who was a member of the congregation. The Baptistry contains a figure of the Good Shepherd by C. d'O. Pilkington Jackson and stained glass windows by Douglas Strachan. The congregation has now been united with that of Christ Church, Trinity.

The Presbyterian Inverleith Church, at the top of Granton Road, was built in 1881 by the Free Church at a cost of £5000 to replace an earlier iron church erected in 1874 on a different site to meet the needs of residents in the then comparatively small number of houses located in Granton and Wardie. The new building was called the St. James Free Church, but this was changed to United Free on the amalgamation of the Free and United Presbyterian Churches in 1900. The final change came nine years later when, as Inverleith Parish Church, it assumed its present status of a congregation of the Church of Scotland, the U.F. churches having then returned to the established fold. During the depression of the 1930s Sunday services for the unemployed were held in the Alhambra Theatre in Leith Walk and a Leith Unemployed Men's Club was started in 1932 with Dr Arthur Cowan, Minister of Inverleith Parish Church, as President.

To the east of Inverleith Row lie the ancient lands of Warriston, and the name 'Warriston House' could until recently, when it was removed on commencement of new housebuilding activity on the site of the old mansionhouse itself, be seen on a solitary, derelict gate-pier standing, like a stout old tree defying the woodman's axe, at the entrance to the Georgian mansion that replaced an earlier house on the same site and was itself demolished, along with the lodge, in the 1960s. As James Grant has remarked, 'Like the house of

Fig. 3. Inverleith Church at the top of Granton Road was built in 1881.

Inverleith, it must have formed a conspicuous object from the once open . . . expanse of Wardie Muir'. The gates of Warriston House, particularly beautiful examples of wrought-iron work, were preserved from destruction during the Second World War by the Best family, the last to live in the house. Some years later they were set up a few feet inside the west entrance to Drummond Place Gardens where they may readily be seen from the street.

A house clearly much older than the others in Inverleith Row, and standing immediately behind an outer wall a short distance northwards from the erstwhile gate-pier, was at one time within the bounds of the Warriston House estate and may well have been a gardener's cottage as it adjoins the remains of a curved wall which was probably part of the walled garden of Warriston House. Considerably altered and enlarged in later years, it dates back to the late eighteenth century, possibly to around the 1780s.

Warriston House was in the possession of the Somervilles in the early sixteenth century, but by the 1580s the Kincaids had succeeded them. In 1600 a dark tragedy took place in the original house. Jean Livingston, the wife of John Kincaid of Warriston, who appears to have been badly treated by her husband, persuaded a servant of her father called Robert Weir to do away with him. Both of them were tried for the murder and sentenced to death. Charles Kirkpatrick Sharpe, who wrote an account of these events, says that the Lady of Warriston, who was only 21, accepted her fate with resignation and in a spirit of great contrition. She was executed by the 'Maiden' at the Girth Cross of Edinburgh, reading an address to the assembled spectators, who were moved to compassion by her serenity and courage, from the scaffold. A later owner was Sir Archibald Johnson, a Lord of Session in 1641, to whom Oliver Cromwell granted a peerage. He took the title of Lord Warriston, but the honour cost him his life as he was executed in Edinburgh after the Restoration of Charles II.

Warriston Crescent, its elegant houses turning their backs on the Water of Leith at 'Puddocky', was built on the Warriston House estate in 1818, and it was here, at No. 10, that Fryderyk Chopin, the Polish composer and musician, stayed in 1848, the year before his death from tuberculosis, when he visited Edinburgh during his last concert tour. A century afterwards a plaque was placed on the wall by the Polish community and their Scottish friends in Edinburgh to commemorate the anniversary. A feature of this area which may have caught Chopin's eye was the toll-house which once stood at the south-west corner of the bridge at Canonmills. Further north, Eildon Street was also built on ground feued from the Warriston estate. A terrace of substantial villas, it

Fig. 4. The oddly named farmhouse of Windlestrawlee, now surrounded by modern houses.

was placed on the perimeter of Warriston Recreation Ground, similarly feued, with the deliberate intention of capitalising on the open view back to the famous skyline of the old city and the First New Town. The site of an ornamental pond is now occupied by tennis courts and the whole playingfield area becomes very readily waterlogged in wet weather. Warriston Cemetery lies to the east, and eastward of it Sir Robert Lorimer's Crematorium has replaced the former East Warriston House, a villa by the nineteenth-century architect, Thomas Bonnar.

On the north side of Ferry Road, northwards and westwards of Inverleith Row, the playing fields, known as

Ferryfield, of the former Melville College for boys were laid out over the fertile soil of Windlestrawlee Farm, quaintly so called after the crested dogtail grass known as windlestrae, a name, says Grant, which was also applied in Scotland to bent and stalks of grass found on moorish ground. A path bordered with white stones leads to the farmhouse, a small, whitewashed, one-storey cottage which is extended as a byre, the difference between the two sections being windows and a chimney in the house and skylights in the byre roof for the animals. The Ferryfield gates were presented by former pupils of the school at their Club centenary in 1965. On the other side of the road the farm of North Inverleith Mains later became the playing fields of Daniel Stewart's College, owned by the Edinburgh Merchant Company. When Melville College amalgamated with Stewart's College, Ferryfield became the property of the Company, who have since sold the eastern portion of the Ferryfield playing fields for building development.

The city's roots may be deep in its native earth, but Edinburgh is far from being a town planted on the plains: so far indeed as to have had a built-in public transport problem from time immemorial, a difficulty later partially overcome by the building of innumerable bridges. Sparing a thought or two for the ups and downs of life at the present day if these levellers of the terrain were suddenly to vanish brings some realisation of what it was like to go hither and yon before they were constructed. But there were no such short cuts to be engineered on the steep slope northwards from the New Town to Inverleith and, even with the addition of a trace horse, it proved to be too stey a brae for the horse trams which carried passengers through the less precipitous streets from the mid-nineteenth century until more sophisticated methods were introduced. The first solution to the problem was found in the 1880s when underground cable traction was installed and operated from a power station in Henderson Row, a building which still survives as a police vehicle pound. From that date until shortly after the end of the First World

War the much maligned cable cars (which, compared to the 'bus, possessed a picturesque dignity more germane to the ocean going liners that reached the height of their demand and popularity at the same time) were hauled up the hillside, breaking down more frequently as time went on, their route taking them along Inverleith Row from Goldenacre to Canonmills and up Hanover Street, and then back in the reverse direction.

In the days before urban development had laid its civilising influence across the Wardie Muir, the northern landscape was one of long views over trees and undulating grassland to the sea, with an occasional farm or country mansion in the middle distance. The Leith River flowed on its hard-working way from the upstream mills (there were about 70 mills as well as tanneries and other industries along its length) to those at Bonnington and the Port. And when the dwellers in the Old Town would fare abroad, they rode on horseback or, having descended by Leith Wynd to the Nor' Loch valley and climbed up on the other side, set out on foot to their destination, Leith itself perhaps, or Stockbridge, or the rich Rocheid farmlands of Inverleith.

CHAPTER 2

Trinity

'ARE you another antiquary?' enquired the local resident, domiciled in one of its modern neighbours, as the camera recorded, in a burst of sunshine, the only surviving remnant of the once large and venerable House of Wardie. Bereft of its principal structural components, it hides its crow-stepped, unassuming dignity and its one remaining graceful seaward turret well out of sight behind the trafficways, the former

Fig. 5. The surviving remnant of the once large and ancient house of Wardie, still used as a private dwellinghouse.

spaciousness of its surroundings now reduced to a tiny fragment of front garden where a few low shrubs and white-helmeted snowdrops were defying the elemental weather on this mad March morning. It was one of those typical 'Edinburgh' days when cold March winds and biting April showers, alternating with a sudden piercing sun, produced Stevenson's 'downright meteorological purgatory' for one half-hour, and June suns and skies of Mediterranean brilliance for the next. 'That's the west wing' (though it is in fact the kitchen premises, left standing when the rest was demolished), went on the local resident, clutching his hat, 'all that's left of the old place. The main, central part was here, where we're standing; it's been gone for donkeys' years. And it took a pitched battle with officialdom to save this final bit from a similar fate about twenty years ago.'

Its age is perhaps not known with certainty, but it was near the old castle of Wardie that, in 1544, the Earl of Hertford landed with an army of ten thousand soldiers. This invading host was sent by Henry VIII 'to burn Edinburgh . . ., to sack Leith', and to put 'man, woman and child to fire and sword', in an attempt to take Mary, the infant Queen of Scots, by force when the treaty with England under which she was betrothed to Edward, Henry's son, went unfulfilled. Hertford was soundly beaten, but a high price was paid in life and property to disengage the Queen, too young to be troubled by the first tumult of her tempestuous life, from this 'rough wooing'. The old fortalice of Wardie, or Granton, is mentioned again in a charter of 1605 when it appears to have been in the possession of Sir John Tours, or Touris, of Inverleith. About fifty years later stones from 'the ruinous manor of Wardie' were being used, along with others from nearby villages, to build Cromwell's Citadel in Leith. It must have been rebuilt, however, as a mansionhouse is known to have been here in 1780, the property of Sir Alexander Boswall of Wardie whose name is perpetuated in Boswall Road.

The short side street opens up at this end into a square bounded by the low walls of another and sharply contrasting

Fig. 6.   Challenger Lodge where navigation charts were drawn up in the
1870s is now St. Columba's Hospice.

house with stiff, Grecian symmetry and a columned portico,
on the other side, standing in greensward as neat and
spreading as Wardie's cottage garden is confined and wild.
'Challenger Lodge,' said my informant, waving his hand in
the direction of the wall. 'There's an interesting story
connected with it. It belonged to a seafaring man in the
nineteenth century — quite a character they say. He was
asked to sail round the world, no less, and then to draw up
navigation charts from the scientific information obtained
during protracted soundings in the seven seas. He came back
here afterwards and wrote it all up, calling the house,
formerly Wardie Lodge, after his ship, *The Challenger.*

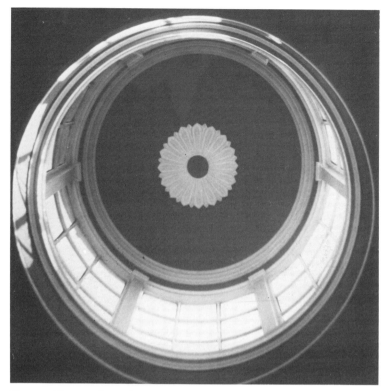

Fig. 7. The cupola in the entrance hall at Challenger Lodge is painted in Pompeian red.

They're still in use today, those charts, so he must have been the right man for the job.' This intrepid mariner was Sir John Murray, K.C.B., F.R.S., who died in 1914, a naturalist with the *Challenger* Expedition of 1872-76, and after that voyage of discovery he edited the reports, which ran to fifty volumes of charts, in this pleasant Grecian house designed by W.H. Playfair in 1825. A home for disabled children for many years, it has now experienced a sea-change into St. Columba's Hospice. The entrance hall has an imposing cupola painted in Pompeian red, a chapel in a cheerful blue and, like so many of its neighbours, rear prospects worthy of a ship at sea.

Westward of this historic enclave, the unsheltered walls of

Fig. 8.   An old anchor from the Siege of Leith outside the former Royal Forth Yacht Club.

the Royal Forth Yacht Club (on the site of the original entrance to Wardie House) have withstood many an equinoctial gale stirred up by the spirits of the Firth who had been early at their boisterous work that morning. A huge anchor has found a peaceful mooring out of the waves' way by the wall in front of the forecourt of the Club, and I leaned over to read the inscription, momentarily bright or darkened by the scudding clouds, as it became decipherable. It had been 'lost during the siege of Leith in 1564 when Queen Elizabeth sent her fleet under Admiral Winter who bombarded Inchkeith which was successfully held by the Scotch and French troops under General Essé'. The anchor was recovered in 1899 by Mr D. Armit and presented by his widow. It might well have been on such a day as this that an armed fleet, on the orders of the redoubtable Protestant Queen, entered the waters of the Firth of Forth or, as it is called on Blaeu's Atlas of 1654, 'Edenburgh Fyrth', for an abortive trial of strength with the island's defenders, and it is not hard to imagine one of them being blown off course and foundering on some rocky coastal defile. Or perhaps, in an attempt to hold the ship at anchor after nightfall, the massive iron hook was fouled by some submerged obstruction from which the vessel had to be cut free at dawn as the ships withdrew from the encounter and made the best of their way back to the open sea. The Royal Forth Yacht Club building has now been converted into flats, and the Club itself has removed to Granton.

Victory in the Reformation wars had been with the Lords of the Congregation in 1560, but not without assistance from the Auld Enemy across the Border, a strange alliance for the Scots, many of whom had supported Mary of Guise, the Queen Regent, who had entrenched herself, and the French soldiery who had been summoned to aid her cause, in the port of Leith. Mary had died in that decisive year of Scotland's history but the tenacious French had continued to garrison the island of Inchkeith until 1567.

Round the corner, entered by the vertical rails through which no creels could pass and long known as the Fishwives' Puzzle, Wardie Steps descend to Granton and sea level at the western extremity of Trinity. Before it was chosen as a 'dormitory suburb' in which to build their streets of gardened villas by the merchants of the Port, it was part of the desolate and extensive Wardie Muir, that undulating wasteland, already mentioned, between Inverleith and the sea, bounded on the east by Bonnington and crossed by the Anchorfield Burn. And much earlier than that, in prehistoric times, glaciers covered the whole area and the sea was far to the east of the Forth valley. It was here, from about the year A.D. 1000, that the monks of Holyrood had their farms, and the

land did not pass out of their ownership till the reign of James IV, who bought it from the Abbot in 1505 to build a harbour at Newhaven. Grant writes of several fragments of human remains being discovered there, along the coast of Wardie, in 1846 when excavations for a bridge of the Granton Railway were being carried out, which appeared to be evidence of the 'occupation of the soil at a very remote period by native tribes'. Silver and copper coins of Spanish origin were also found, and tales were rife of 'some great galleon' from the Armada which had been 'cast away upon the rocky coast'.

In July 1558, when the marriage of the Queen of Scots to the French Dauphin, this time an unopposed and peaceful if short-lived alliance, was celebrated in her native country, ten shillings Scots was paid to the pioneers who fired the Royal Salute from Mons Meg, that legendary piece of ordnance at the Castle, and the 'bullet' (in those days 'shotted guns' were sometimes used on such occasions) was afterwards retrieved two miles away at Wardie Muir. But all that was a long while since, and the rough old moor has been suburbanised and tamed out of existence.

Opposite the Georgian porticos of Trinity Crescent, feued about 1824 when sea bathing was becoming popular in Trinity and before the sands of Portobello superseded it, the Chain Pier had been built out into the water. It was designed by a man called Parrot and cost £4000. The pier was constructed in 1821 and, when King George IV paid his famous visit to Scotland the following year, it was considered as a possible disembarkation point, instead of The Shore at Leith, for 'the sacred foot of Majesty'. But Trinity had to forego that honour; the claims of Leith to be the royal port of entry for the nation were too well founded to be set aside. It did, however, receive the feet of a very different and this time departing king, the exiled and abdicated Charles X of France. Pursued by his creditors, he had been welcomed to Holyrood Palace under its ancient rights of sanctuary from debt, but in 1832, with old-style, pre-Revolution monarchy anathema in France and the newly passed Reform Act decreasing his popularity in Edinburgh, he and his household stepped from the Chain Pier on to a steam packet bound for Hamburg on the 18th of September. He had become an anachronism in his own lifetime and died five years afterwards, aged 79.

The Chain Pier was used by steamdriven boats plying up and down the River Forth but, not being suitable for large vessels, was soon abandoned for the advantages of Granton Harbour. 'Great swimming Competitions' were held frequently at the Chain Pier on Saturdays and were conspicuously advertised in the local newspaper. It eventually fell into decay and was finally swept off in a storm around the end of last century. The Chain Pier Bar now occupies the building which was once the booking office.

In the third quarter of the eighteenth century, when the New Town of Edinburgh was abuilding, the 'sylvan suburb' of Trinity was a pleasant stretch of countryside on the shores of Forth with all the makings of a fine, healthful holiday resort. It was not unnatural therefore that those who could afford to leave their tumbling tenements and needier neighbours in the old, overcrowded city for a new town house of space and grace in the very new New Town should see in Trinity the ideal situation for their country villas. Nor had its qualities gone unobserved by the no less affluent merchants and shipowners of the Port. For them, it was an obvious and even more convenient place of potential residence. So the ground which the Fraternity of Masters and Mariners of Trinity House, which stands in the Kirkgate in Leith, had bought in 1713 from Evan MacGregor (who may well have been Welsh on his mother's side as he changed his name to Evan Evans), the King's — or more appropriately the Queen's as Queen Anne's reign did not end till the following year — Bailiff by whom the land was administered for the Crown, became the site of active, and in some cases during the Victorian period one might be forgiven for suspecting pretentious, private building operations.

The Trinity House officials had been responsible for laying

B

Fig. 9. Trinity House in the Kirkgate opposite South Leith Church contains memorabilia of the Fraternity of Masters and Mariners of Leith. It replaced an older building on the same site in 1816.

out the farm of Trinity Mains which had in time given its name to the whole area. The adoption of Trinity as a place name is explained by the fact that Leith, in common with other ports throughout the United Kingdom, had dedicated its charitable institution to the Holy Trinity and had called its headquarters and subsequently its farm by that name which then, as streets and houses were erected, came to be used for the entire district. Some part of the old farmhouse of Trinity Mains is said to have been incorporated in the later, but now demolished, farmhouse of Hay Lodge in East Trinity Road. This later house, surrounded by trees and closed in by a wall, was surmounted by a half-timbered tower, and in the garden was an ancient vinery with eighteen vines. In the late nineteenth and early twentieth centuries this was the home of Mr Graham-Yooll, a man much addicted to sporting activities, who kept and raced several greyhounds and indulged in the dubious pastime of cock-fighting, for which a room in the house was set aside. He was well known at the time as owner of the Gaiety Theatre in Leith and also of part of the Marine Gardens, then a place of popular amusement, dancing and indoor roller-skating in Portobello. The house was known for a time as Dulham Tower, Dulham being the name of a later owner, who was manager of the Standard Life Assurance Company in Edinburgh, but it reverted to its original name of Hay Lodge in 1936.

Apart from fragments such as Wardie House, the oldest surviving house in Trinity is Trinity Lodge, at the foot of Stirling Road, built in 1774 by Robert Johnston, an Edinburgh merchant, but it is now flatted and has a modern house in its much reduced grounds, a fate that has befallen a number of properties in the district. But by far the most interesting, and probably the most secluded, dwelling is the slightly later Trinity Grove in Trinity Road, built by David Hunter of Blackness in Angus, whose son Alexander was a partner in the publishing firm of Constable & Co., in 1790. The house is described in the Scottish Development Department's official listing as 'simple late Georgian vernacular' and still stands where it did, though it is now surrounded by later additions which include a tower, probably erected in a last desperate attempt to obtain the view, so beloved by the early Trinity villa builders, over the chimney stacks of its proliferating neighbours. Unlike Trinity Lodge, it no longer bears its original name and, along with a beautiful garden, is well enclosed by its walls; only a glimpse can be caught from outside of intriguing features such as stone urns and roof-top iron storks.

Alexander Hunter was bought out of Constable's company in 1811 and died the following year, the little villa being sold

Fig. 10.   Trinity Lodge, built in 1774 and the oldest surviving house in Trinity.

to William Creech as a summer residence. Mr Creech was well known in Edinburgh as bookseller, publisher and Lord Provost. His shop, previously owned by Allan Ramsay, was in Creech's Land in the Luckenbooths beside St. Giles, and Chambers writes of these premises as a 'Lounger's Observatory, for seldom was the doorway free of some group of idlers . . . Creech himself, with his black silk breeches and powdered head, being ever a conspicuous member of the corps'. Perhaps because of his advancing years, he made no alterations to the house and concentrated his attention on the garden, growing fruit and vegetables with the assistance of a gardener. When he died unmarried in 1815 Trinity Grove, continuing its literary connections, passed to John Ballantyne, the most interesting and by far the most flamboyant of its owners and brother of the more famous James who was printer and, to their mutual undoing, business collaborator of Sir Walter Scott.

John was by this time an auctioneer with premises in Hanover Street which he later removed to Waterloo Place. He himself had a fine collection of *objets d'art* at Trinity Grove, which was rechristened 'Harmony Hall' during his incumbency, but most noteworthy were his 'portraits of beautiful actresses' such as Pegg Woffington and Kitty Clive, as John Gibson Lockhart points out in his *Life of Scott*. The ebullient auctioneer made a practice of entertaining the famous theatrical personalities of the day at Harmony Hall when they had engagements in Edinburgh, and actors as famous as Kean, Braham and Kemble displayed their talents for the enjoyment of John and his guests, among whom Scott and Constable were frequently included. Besides his table furnished with many delicacies, John Ballantyne's stable was no less well provided, and he 'usually rode up to his auction on a tall milk-white hunter, yclept Old Mortality, attended by a leash or two of greyhounds'.

He built a large addition to the house about 1816, more than doubling its size, and it is on the roof of the Ballantyne part (now a separate house) that the storks and urns, best seen from the garden at the back, provide interest and embellishment. To his extended residence he attached a wing for his own personal use, and in order to keep out his wife — 'the handsome and portly lady', as Lockhart called her, 'who bore his name' — he had the entrances made so narow that she could not 'force her person through any one of them'. The auctioneer, being small and consumptive, had no such difficulty. He was given to playing on a French horn 'with an energy by no means prudent in the state of his lungs', and as early as 1821, when he was only forty-seven, his name appears for the last time in the Post Office Directories as the owner of Trinity Grove. But the 'villa near to the Firth' had witnessed the colourful, though brief, enactment of a rich slice of Edinburgh history as the home of just such a thriftless but kenspeckle character as only her 'golden age' could have thrown up.

Later in the nineteenth century Trinity Grove belonged to Richard Mackie, a self-made man equally typical of his time. Born in Dunfermline, at an early age he joined a firm of shipbrokers in Leith and thus embarked on a career which was to lead him straight to financial success and civic honour. In 1873, before he was twenty-five, he had become sole proprietor and, going into partnership with his brother-in-law, steered the business into coal exporting as Mackie, Koth & Co. The firm of Richard Mackie & Co., Shipowners, was founded in 1882. He was three times Provost of Leith, and on his receiving a knighthood in June 1909 the *Leith Observer* devoted considerable space to an account of his life, with photographs of himself and his wife. A bust of Sir Richard had been commissioned 'to adorn the vestibule of Leith Town Hall', and tribute was paid to all he had done 'to sweeten the relationship between the Corporations of Edinburgh and Leith'.

In 1927 the house was subdivided, and the southern part of the garden ground became the building site for a western extension of East Trinity Road. An interesting booklet, *The Story of an Old Edinburgh House*, giving historical details of Trinity Grove, has been writen by Mr R. L. Hunter, F.S.A., F.S.A.Scot.

According to Grant, 'Horatio MacCulloch, R.S.A., the well-known landscape painter, lived latterly in a villa adjoining Trinity Grove, and died there on the 15th June 1867'.

South Trinity Road and Trinity Road are the original road to Trinity, and the irregular line of the latter is due to its having been drawn round the edge of the fields as it wound northwards towards the sea. To the west of Trinity Grove, on the opposite side of the street, was Trinity Hut, an example of the small (though they were sometimes quite spacious

Georgian houses) summer retreats built on the then city outskirts, usually by the owners of large town mansions, another example being Leith Mount which has been superseded on its site by Leith Town Hall and Public Library at the eastern end of Ferry Road. Yet another called Lilypot was where the Telephone Exchange now stands in Clark Road. Houses for permanent, year-round residence came later, especially after the advent of the railway.

Trinity Hut was the home, in the eighteenth century, of a French émigré called Pierre de la Motte who had decided to set up a school of dancing in Edinburgh. As a master of the Terpsichorean art, he achieved the unlikely notoriety of getting on the wrong side of the law on several occasions. In 1742 John Mitchell of Windlestrawlee made complaints to the Burlaw Court in Leith to the effect that de la Motte was 'overrunning his cornfields' when out hunting, the offending hunting party consisting of eight or nine gentlemen and 'twa dogs'. The outcome of the case does not appear to have been recorded and, indeed, it may never have been heard because the defendant calmly sent a friend to tell the Court he was unable to attend as the hearing coincided with his dancing lessons. Two years later he was again brought before the Burlaw Court, this time accused of filling in a ditch opposite Lilypot, and in yet another brush with authority he was charged with making off with his neighbour's 'fulzie', or manure, to fertilise his own ground at Trinity Hut. This over-enthusiastic if many-sided character was a keen gardener, and his 'evergreen oaks' are said to have been a feature of this part of Trinity till long after his own time.

In August 1847 the Danish poet and writer of children's tales, Hans Christian Andersen, then in middle age and on a short visit to Edinburgh, stayed with Joseph Hambro, a member of the banking family whose name has been carried down to modern times in financial circles, at the now demolished Lixmount House which had been built in 1794 by an Edinburgh Writer to the Signet whose wife had come from the little village of Lix Toll in Perthshire. The village gave its name to their new residence, and the site of the former entrance lodge is marked today by the medical practice located in The Long House at 73 East Trinity Road. In the early years of the nineteenth century Lixmount was the residence of the Farquharsons of Invercauld. The house known as Christian Bank, pulled down after an existence of only eighty years, was built by the Danish Consul in 1768 and named after King Christian VII.

In the northern section of Trinity Road, after the opening of the branch railway line, Christian Bank lay between the station and the house called Primrose Bank which is still in residential occupation as Shirley Lodge in Primrose Bank Road to which it gave its name.

Towards the sea, on the Laverockbank estate, Sir James Young Simpson, whose name is more usually associated with his town residence at 52 Queen Street, built a house called Inverforth for his maiden sister. This house, set well back within its garden, still survives. Next door, as a country retreat for himself, and because he thought the sea air would be beneficial to his children whose health was a cause of some concern, he bought the eighteenth-century cottage which, together with his considerable additions to it, is now known as Strathavon Lodge. It was here that he hoped eventually to spend his retirement, but the excessive and diverse activities to which his brilliant mind drove him continuously, and his many strength-consuming acts of philanthropy, brought his remarkable and benevolent life to an end when he was only fifty-nine. Simpson himself extended the original cottage, then and during his lifetime known as Viewbank, with what amounted to a larger house built on at the back and overlooking the sea. This was further enlarged by the addition of an extra storey by a later owner at the end of the nineteenth century.

In the garden is the reclining figure of a dog carved in stone and traditionally thought to represent the same animal which the doctor used to assist him in his experiments with chloroform, but there is no documentary evidence for this natural, though possibly incorrect, assumption. Simpson's coach-house and stable are still there, and the wild garden with its rough, coarse grass still growing as it did in bygone centuries, is a surviving, virgin fragment of the ancient Wardie Muir. A long, narrow, grass-grown level area is said to have been Simpson's bowling green. This accords with Cockburn's recollection, mentioned in his *Memorials*, of long, smooth lanes of turf, anciently called bowling alleys, in the garden of Prestonfield House, the home of his father's friend, Sir William Dick of Prestonfield.

In her account of her father's life, Eve Blantyre Simpson recalls the purchase of the house in Trinity and how it had become imperative for him from time to time to 'escape from the sound of the never-silent doorbell at No. 52'. Here he would enjoy for supper 'tea, an egg and a sunset' before retiring for an undisturbed night's sleep. Crossing from Burntisland one day in the company of a visitor from the East, he was informed that the scenery of the Bosphorus was as nothing compared with that of the Forth opposite Granton! Hans Andersen was among the numerous distinguished foreigners entertained by Dr Simpson. Anyone staying in the house today is said to sleep with exceptional soundness. The explanation is that it is due to the influence of Simpson and his chloroform!

William Wilde, Irish father of the more famous Oscar, knew Simpson well and was, like him, a keen archaeologist and enquirer into natural phenomena. Sir James once asked for his opinion on the placing of a telescope on the roof of Viewbank in pursuance of his amateur astronomical studies, but Wilde successfully discouraged him, maintaining that its purpose would be defeated by the Edinburgh weather!

When the name of this historic house was changed it became Strathavon Lodge because the doctor, a native of Bathgate and of Huguenot descent on his mother's side, had chosen to be known as Sir James Young Simpson of Strathavon on receiving his baronetcy. He died at 52 Queen Street in 1870 and was buried in Warriston Cemetery, his

Fig. 11.   Christ Church, Trinity, once a private chapel and now a private house.

family deciding on a last resting place beside that of his children who had predeceased him, although a tomb in Westminster Abbey had been proposed. A portrait medallion was placed there to his memory instead.

Opposite Strathavon Lodge is Starbank Park, created in the late nineteenth century from the gardens of Laverockbank and Starbank Houses, James Simpson, the Leith architect, having been employed to lay out the grounds, where a star-shaped flowerbed embellishes the bank. The house of Starbank was the home of The Rev. Walter M. Goalen who built, at his own expense, the Episcopal Christ Church at the corner of Trinity Road and Primrose Bank Road, the pulpit of

Fig. 12. Laverockbank Cottage was originally the Lodge of the demolished Laverockbank House.

which he occupied himself. This graceful little church with its spire among trees was designed by John Henderson in 1854 and was a private chapel for twenty or thirty years before being taken over by the Scottish Episcopal Church. It has been transformed in recent years into a dwellinghouse, the congregation having amalgamated with that of St. James's at Goldenacre. Starbank House, classically symmetrical in design, is ornamented with neo-Gothic detail and has now been converted into two flats for employees of the Parks Department of Edinburgh District Council. In the spring gales of 1982 the old retaining park wall in Laverockbank Road, its cement no doubt eroded by the frosts of many a severe winter

Fig. 13.   Starbank House and Park. The house is a larger version of
Laverockbank Cottage and was probably built around the same time.

long gone by, was blown down and collapsed in a rickle of
stones. The charming old wall has been carefully rebuilt, and
it is to be hoped that this will act as a salutary conservation
precedent.

The street known as Mayville Gardens takes its name from
Mayville House which is pleasantly situated next to the Park
in Laverockbank Road. It would appear to have been built as
the dower house for Laverockbank House. The name of this
large tall-standing residence was changed to Bankhead many
years ago.

Laverockbank House, approached from the seaward road
on the north, was an early eighteenth-century villa with a

long, low, trellised addition built across the north front early in the following century and was noted for its oval library. The entrance was probably moved to the other, East Trinity Road, side when the house was enlarged. This interesting building was unfortunately demolished around 1938. The lodge, now called Laverockbank Cottage, on the south side and probably built when the extension was added to the house, has been spared and stands, obliquely out of line with the rest of the street, in the eastern section of East Trinity Road. An interesting feature is the prominent round projection at the back, which may be a stair tower, and there is a tiny garden to the front. This little house presents to the street a frontage which, with its broad, oversailing eaves and 'Gothic'-arched doorway, bears too strong a resemblance to Starbank Park House for this to have been accidental. It is likely that they were both built not only at about the same time but, as many of the Trinity villas were, by the same builder. Its fortunate survival adds considerable interest and character to its surroundings.

Of even greater interest is a group of old houses and cottages further west in Boswall Road. Well back from the street and hiding among trees stands Earnock, the oldest part of which was probably built in the seventeenth century and the newest around the end of the nineteenth. Known originally as West Cottage, it was built, along with three others, on the estate of Wardie House. Nearby is the sixteenth-century South Cottage, an example of a 'but and ben' with an eighteenth-century extension. East Cottage, next door, was the Wardie coach house, and it is on record that it was once the home of 'Christopher North'. At the end of Boswall Road three conjoined houses, Boswall House, Wardiebank House and Manor House, form an interesting group. They belonged to Sir Donald Pollock, a former Chancellor of Edinburgh University, who lived in the Manor House while the other two became the Pollock Missionary Residences. The external ironwork is noteworthy as it is said to have come from the liner *Aquitania* and incorporates the ornamental letter 'A' in several places. The poet and essayist, Alexander Smith, lived in one of the Boswall Road villas, and wrote of the great city to which he looked out every morning in his lines on a 'Vision of Edinburgh as seen from Trinity'. Born at Kilmarnock on 31st December 1829, he died on 5th February 1869 and was buried in Warriston Cemetery where a Celtic cross with a portrait medallion on the shaft was erected to his memory. The grave is near the eastern entrance. Also interred at Warriston are Horatio McCulloch, R.S.A., Adam Black the publisher, Sir James Young Simpson, M.D., and Robert Scott Lauder, R.S.A., his tomb bearing a medallion portrait sculpted by J. Hutchison, R.S.A.

Wardie Church, on its corner site in Primrose Bank Road, was built in 1893.

The Victorian predilection for cottages no doubt prompted the name of the tall, baronial-type mansion built on the southern flank of Trinity at Goldenacre (once known, because of its fertility in contrast to the stubborn, unproductive moor, as Goldenriggs) as recently as 1894 by the Leith shipowning family of Currie by whom it was put latterly to business use. Architecturally, Trinity Cottage looked backward to an earlier Scottish building style (like the picturesque row of riverside almshouses, of identical date and mediaeval in conception down to the commemorative donor's tablet on the streetfacing gable, at Coltbridge) rather than forward to the space-age, synthetic functionalism that was to work out its urban destiny in the twentieth century. Trinity Cottage was the successor of a cottage to which the name originally and appropriately belonged and which can be seen on some nineteenth-century maps of the district. Around 1830 it was the home of the farmer at Windlestrawlee a short distance to the west in Ferry Road. The subsequent mansionhouse, rearing its crow-stepped heights among trees that were noted for their age and beauty, rose grandly above a well-kept hedge to look out, in Spring, on a carpet of lush grass and crocuses.

It was a high, cold old house, as a descendant of the Currie

Fig. 14. Trinity Cottage at Goldenacre in the Spring of 1969 shortly before its demolition. It had been the home of the Currie family who founded the Currie Line.

family wrote in 1968, recalling her memories of the 1920s, with a long drawing-room and a huge fireplace which could accommodate yard-long logs in a room at the top of the building. When her great-aunt, who lived there latterly alone with a 'kind, sandy-haired maid who stood like a grenadier in her white cap and apron', died, the mansion became a home for babies. During the Second World War the children were evacuated and the premises turned over to office use by the Currie Line. The gardens of Trinity Cottage and the turreted, dormer-windowed Larkfield were opened to the public on Sunday, 16th May 1954, under Scotland's Gardens Scheme.

On the west side of the estate, and entered from Wardie Road, Larkfield had been in existence for some time when Trinity Cottage was built. Although of secondary importance after the advent of the larger building, it was nevertheless of considerable interest and was rebuilt to the designs of the architect Hippolyte Blanc in the late nineteenth century, its red roofs contrasting with the more sombre later mansion.

Thanks to the onward march of progress, this beautiful small estate has been redeveloped, and the only buildings left are the lodges at the entrance gate to Larkfield in Wardie Road, now, happily, restored and occupied by an architectural practice. A few token trees, much older than the buildings themselves, were permitted to remain, but as for the rest — like the gowk, redevelopers hae nae sang but ane! The curving walls of Trinity Park House, currently occupied by the Inland Revenue, now spread their artstone banality across the site.

Nonetheless, Trinity remains remarkably unspoiled in comparison with other places and, if Scott and Constable and the brothers Ballantyne could walk today down the streets they knew so well, they would probably be well able to recognise it even though they would find its rural character greatly changed. An aura of history, and the individuality of its Georgian and Victorian houses and their mature gardens, make it still one of the most charming and attractive residential districts of the city in spite of the inevitable, and indeed desirable, intrusion of some new building into the area not all of which, however, has been designed to blend with its environment.

The house of Newbank lay immediately to the north of Trinity Cottage, and beyond it was the more extensive ground, with its Georgian residence, Rose Park, well away from the street, which was auctioned by Dowells (now Phillips in Scotland) of George Street along with 1.6 acres of land in 1962 for building purposes. All that remains (as is so frequently the case) is the gate-piered entrance with the name 'Rose Park' still readable in fading white paint on one of the stones.

It was at Mayfield House in East Trinity Road that Mr Christian Salvesen lived. A Norwegian, he came to Scotland when he was sixteen years of age and entered a shipbroking firm in Glasgow. After spending some time in Germany and his native Norway, he returned to Edinburgh in 1851 and joined his brother in the business of Salvesen & Turnbull. His own shipping concern, Christian Salvesen & Co., came later and his three sons, all born in Leith, went into their father's employment there. A fourth son became Lord Salvesen, a Senator of the College of Justice. Christian Salvesen died in Mayfield House in January 1911, aged 83, and was buried in Rosebank Cemetery, laid out on the grounds of the demolished house of that name at the corner of Pilrig Street and Bonnington Road. The house of Denham Green, in Clark Road, was given by this family to the Edinburgh Academy and is still in use as its preparatory school. On John Ainslie's map of 1804 Denham Green is shown as the property of Sir Henry Moncrieff, and it was a residence of the Earl of Caithness in the 1830s.

In the angle between the two houses of Mayfield and Denham Green, Earl Haig Gardens can be reached by taking the approach path from East Trinity Road. This First World War Settlement was one of many organised by the Scottish Veterans' Garden City Association for disabled ex-servicemen and their families, and the site was obtained by the Leith Committee from the Salvesens, who curtailed their own grounds in order to accommodate the settlement. Thirty-one flatted villas were then built round a grass-centred square, Field Marshall Earl Haig, K.T., performing the opening ceremony on 1st October 1921. An inscribed stone in the wall at East Trinity Road is beside the entrance, and carved tablets can be seen on some of the houses, commemorating the sons of local families, including the Salvesens, who fell in action. On a wet July day in 1923 this settlement was visited by King George V and Queen Mary when a special pavilion was erected for their official reception. After touring the houses and talking with the men and their wives and children, the

Fig. 15.   Lomond House stands at the slope's top in York Road and looks out across the Firth of Forth.

Queen planted a tree in a corner of the square to mark the occasion.

Returning to East Trinity Road, the usual remnant of an entrance gate was left standing when Trinity House, a central block with later, nineteenth-century, additions on either side, was demolished in 1978. The proliferation of modern housing now occupying the site is in stark contrast to the beautiful Georgian dwellings behind their mature, well-cultivated gardens, on the other side, two stone-carved owls, perpetually perched in imminent flight, above the gate of Rose Cottage, being a particularly pleasing and well-preserved street asset. These individually designed houses are of exceptional merit and attractiveness, and of equal distinction are Grecian Cottage in Lennox Row and Gothic House round the corner in York Road where the high-standing, far-viewing Lomond House is poised above its entrance archways at the steep slope's top. At the slope's top too is Woodbine Cottage, shrinking away, as well it might, from public gaze, for this little eighteenth-century house, set well back in its garden, was at one time a smugglers' cottage and has an underground passageway leading down to the sea. An iron ring in one of the floor boards could once be pulled up to gain entrance to the secret tunnel, but this has now been floored over and there is no longer any possibility of access being obtained at the other end, as it has been completely blocked up by later buildings across the opening. The existence of this pirates' passage could now be forgotten (and overlooked by anyone studying local history in the future), and it is possible that it may have been filled in at the lower, or sea, end during building and road-making operations.

About 1835 Trinity House of Leith began feuing the ground at Laverockbank Road, but the short line of villas and gardens at the south-east end was not continued further although this was originally intended. On the opposite side of the street, the house on the corner of Laverockbank Road (and next door to Woodville described in the following chapter) provides an example of the vicissitudes which individual dwelling-houses can experience. Built around the early 1830s, it can be traced on old maps of the Trinity area as having started life with the name of Spring Cottage, going on to become successively Ramsay Cottage and then The Cottage. Finally, following conversion to upper and lower flats at the end of the Second World War, it ended up with two separate street numbers in Laverockbank and East Trinity Roads.

As interesting examples of the wide variety of architectural styles indulged in in Victorian times, Gothic House in York Road and Grecian Cottage in Lennox Row have been already mentioned, as has also Lomond House standing proud on its

Fig. 16.   The house formerly known as The Cottage at the corner of Laverockbank Road *c.* 1910.

Fig. 17.   The house in Fig. 16 as it looks today converted into upper and lower flats.

Fig. 18. Gothic House, one of many interestingly designed houses in 19th century Trinity.

commanding height with a fashionable tower, ensuring its owners an uninterrupted view well beyond the Lomond Hills, its garden and the one next door entered through twin round-headed arches from the street. There are gables, imitation English half-timbering, romantic cottages that have grown as greater space was needed into substantial houses, and gate lodges and little carriage drives as well. Pretentious? At the time perhaps, but what a rare environmental legacy to the generations that were to come!

A little rustic building known as Goldenacre Cottage stood for many years on the south-east side of South Trinity Road, but this has long since disappeared.

It is not always realised that Trinity had its own railway station which was entered from York Road, where recent house-building operations have obliterated all that remained on that side. It can, however, be approached from Trinity Crescent, and it is worth while going to have a look at the old platform with its lived-in railway cottages overlooking the line. The trains left Canal Street Station on the site of the later Waverley Market (now also vanished from the scene) and were cable-hauled through a tunnel to Scotland Street Station. From there some of them went, usually every quarter of an hour, to Bonnington and then North Leith Station at the Citadel, and others were detached and run to Trinity and Granton for the Fife ferry which had the distinction of being the first train ferry in the world. The Scotland Street tunnel route was closed in 1868 on the opening of a new line through Abbeyhill to Trinity and Bonnington. It had only been in use for about twenty years, but as it passed beneath Drummond Place in the Second New Town, it had necessitated the demolition of the Georgian mansion of Bellevue, by then the Excise Office, because of the danger of subsidence.

The former Lodge Trinity No. 885 was founded in the closing years of the nineteenth century in 'purpose-built' premises at the foot of Wardie Road. Many local functions were held here, including the annual dances of the still extant Lomond Park Tennis Club which played a prominent part in the social life of Trinity in the years before the First World War. The Lodge, vacated by the recently departed Masons, has been redesigned for residential purposes, and thus another chapter of Trinity history has been brought to an end.

Tradition and local 'characters' persisted in Trinity, as elsewhere, into the early years of the twentieth century. Prior to 1914 the aged Russian Consul to the Port of Leith, who had his house in Lennox Row, was often to be seen pacing up and down the pavement beside his garden wall, carrying a stool on which he sat down for a rest periodically outside his gate. A few four-in-hands and carriages were still in use by some of the inhabitants, including the Salvesens of Mayfield House, now a Cheshire Home, and the Sandersons of Trinity House who drove out in their carriage with a groom at the back blowing a long French horn as they progressed to Princes Street in style. Troughs for watering the tradesmen's and cab-drivers' hard-working animals were a common sight on the streets of Edinburgh, as also, unfortunately, were fallen horses, especially in winter weather when sacks were usually placed on the road for the horses' hooves to stand on when pulled up. Newbank in South Trinity Road, the home of one of Sir Richard Mackie's sons, was one of the last houses where a dogcart, very smart with brightly painted wheels, was kept, behind which a Dalmatian dog used to run when on the road. Colourful and stylish, these times have come and gone, and probably the least changing feature in the landscape is the old Edenburgh Fyrth itself — forby the Edinburgh weather.

'What a dreadful day!' said a passer-by on the pavement, holding her umbrella squarely into a squall. 'Terrible!' I replied, and took a firmer grip on the camera which was now replete with azure skies and the sun-drenched stones of Trinity. Then the March wind caught the dark, bare, winter branches of the trees and shook them roundly, as if impatient for the first green hint of leaves. And suddenly the sun blazed out across the brown earth rich with snowdrops in the gardens, and for a few bright moments it was Spring.

CHAPTER 3

Woodville — A Hidden House

WOODVILLE is a hidden house in a concealed and quiet garden. When you take a summer walk down East Trinity Road the long, high wall to the left of the pavement will give no clue to its existence behind the lawns and ancient trees that extend the garden far back from the street and public scrutiny. Nor will you fare better at the entrance gate in Laverockbank Road where the dark lime- and sycamore-lined

Fig. 19.   The old walls and trees of Laverockbank Road where it slopes steeply towards the sea.

Fig. 20.   The little Regency house of Woodville in its garden near the top of Laverockbank Road.

avenue leads to the side of the house, the eastern wall emerging only gradually from the dark tree shadows, like the 'tunnel of green gloom' in Rupert Brooke's 'Grantchester', as you approach it down the gravel path. But when you walk out onto the grass, in front of the classical garden urns at either side and the great circular rosebed (filled with crocuses in Spring) in the centre, you are confronted by the beautiful and well-proportioned simplicity of a Georgian mansion in miniature which delights and surprises by its very unexpectedness.

The only ornamental feature of this most charming of Trinity villas is the entrance, where the delicate, white-painted astragals of the segmental fanlight above it set off the two sturdy Tuscan columns flanking the doorway itself. Even the rhones have been banished to the north and west sides so that nothing should detract from the plain regularity of the exterior which had, nevertheless, one very unusual feature undetectable from the front of the house. The upper storey was confined to the south-facing frontage and was not continued above the rooms at the back of the building. This trim little villa among the trees, so aptly named by those who built it, can however command one view more distant than a glimpse of tenements to the south and some recent (and incompatible) housing to the immediate north, for the enduring slopes of Arthur's Seat raise their extinct volcanic mass just high enough to the south-east to be discernible.

The steeply slanting ground here above the Forth was known as Laverock Bank on account of the large number of larks — 'laverock is but lark writ large' — which 'came hither in snow', but none is to be heard today. These blithe little songbirds were sold in nearby Newhaven as delicacies for the table and were fortuitously saved from that fate when their habitat was taken over by the villa builders. They are said to have 'migrated to the Solway' but, wherever they may have gone, their name, as euphonious as their song, is all that remains in Trinity as their memorial. Maurice Trent, a merchant in Leith, had bought the land here from the Crown in 1660 and called it Larkbank. This was changed to Laverockbank when it was purchased by Patrick Anderson, a Leith wine cooper, in 1748. The eastern section of Laverockbank was later given the name of Cherry Bank.

1816 is a likely building date for Woodville, which has all the appearance of a little Regency house, and it was on the first day of May in that year that the southmost half as divided and marked off by a thorn hedge of the lot or piece of ground in the West Park of Laverockbank (that is, the level land at the top of the slope) was sold to John Stewart who was thereby bound to pay a proportion of Minister's stipend and King's cess (tax) with other public and parochial burdens, these being the usual obligations undertaken on the acquisition of property. As it was situated sufficiently close to the Firth, however, he was also obliged to pay his share of defending the East, West and Middle Parks of Laverockbank against encroachment by the sea. There was to be no manufactory or other operation carried on on the grounds or any work erected which might be a nuisance. When Kirkwood drew his map of Edinburgh in 1817, the name of 'Mr. Stewart' was printed across the area of which he had become proprietor, but it is possible that the house had been built a few years earlier by the previous owner whose name of Anderson can be seen on maps predating that of Kirkwood. In the Scottish Development Department's List of Buildings of Special Architectural or Historic Interest, Woodville is stated to be of early nineteenth-century date. At all events, it harks back to the period at the end of the Napoleonic Wars, a time when Martello towers had been erected round the coasts of Britain, including one at Leith Docks, as fears of a French invasion ran high throughout the country. The avenue of trees which leads to the house has the reputation of having been planted to commemorate the famous victory of Waterloo in 1815.

For fifty-five years Woodville was the home of John Paris, a native of Bo'ness who, in 1924, purchased it from the Morgan family, one of whose daughters, the painter Miss Annie Morgan, was President of the Scottish Society of Women Artists during the 1940s. Vigorous and active to the end of a ripe old age, Mr. Paris here pursued the two great interests of a many-faceted career — gardening and chemistry. In his younger years he worked as a scientist with the Government Laboratory, travelled in Canada and Russia and held an appointment with the old Excise Department of the Inland Revenue. At Woodville he enlarged and recreated the garden, concentrating mainly on rhododendrons and many varieties of roses, although it was never without colour from early Spring to Autumn. Towards the end of his exceptionally long life the only assistance he would accept was with cutting the grass of the long, spreading lawn which stretches from a few feet in front of the house right down to the beds of roses, delphiniums and dahlias at the other end. Two tall, branching deodars (Cedrus Deodara from the Himalayas, the 'divine Tree' of the Indian poets) planted by him over forty years ago have matured among the older trees in this tree-sheltered garden, and he pointed out in particular to visitors a small-leafed weeping birch of a rare beauty and delicacy, the silver bark rising through the gently drooping branches. An attractive painting of this tree by W. Wight Pringle hung in one of the bedrooms, and another by the same artist of the house was in the entrance hall. These gentle trees contrast noticeably with the strong, dark foliage of the drive, and one remembers that the sycamore is the old 'dool tree' of Scotland from whose branches often hung the mortal remains of thieves and malefactors, while the lime was the tree ecclesiastical, creating, it has been said, a lofty 'Gothic' nave when planted in avenues.

In the May of his ninety-seventh year, in the month of the rhododendron-flowering, Mr Paris conducted a party of seventy members of the Caledonian Horticultural Society around the garden, which covers three-quarters of an acre and was the scene of occasional fêtes and outdoor functions during the summer. In May 1972 it was the subject of an illustrated article in the magazine *Garden News*. Fortunate in its raised situation near the Forth, it is equally fortunate in being just too distant from the water to be adversely affected by the salt sea-spray.

John Paris liked to accompany the interested visitor into the house and up the curving staircase, with wrought-ironwork identical to similar stairways in the New Town which date from much the same period. He had brought, he explained, the white-painted Dutch mantelpiece, probably about three hundred years old, and carved in high relief with flowers, shells and graceful female figures, from an old house in Bo'ness on his removal to Trinity, a house which had originally been the little town's tolbooth and in which one of

Fig. 21. A Spring scene of Woodville house and garden.

the last trials for witchcraft to be held in Scotland had taken place when six women and one man had been sentenced to death. The Bo'ness mantelpiece fitted to perfection round the fireplace in one of the Woodville bedrooms.

In the drawing-room downstairs, to the left of the doorway, is an original mantelshelf, with shallower floral carving, inserted when the house was built. This room was furnished by Mr Paris with an admirable restraint which enabled each piece of furniture, dating appropriately from the late eighteenth or early nineteenth century, to be seen to advantage, including a Georgian writing desk, faded and polished into the beautiful patina of old mahogany, and an oval table of the Adam era decorated with typical paterae and husks. The house contains two false doors, placed, to preserve the interior symmetry of drawing- and dining-rooms, in walls where insufficient thickness was available to provide for cupboard recesses and, opening the genuine six-panelled door in the deeper wall to the left of the drawing-room fireplace, John Paris, or his housekeeper, Miss Hunter, would reveal its treasures — the christening cup made, when Mr Paris was born, at a Glasgow pottery with which his family had for several generations been connected and hand-painted with flowers and the inscription 'John Paris born 13th January 1879'; a glazed earthenware water-bottle with the initials J P and the date 1791 cut into the glaze by the brother of Mr Paris's grandfather and, most interesting of all, an old snuff box found by his great-great-grandfather on the site at Bo'ness where one of Prince Charles's Highland Regiments had encamped on their way to link up with the Jacobite Army before the Battle of Prestonpans in 1745. On the other side of the hall is the dining-room, the only room in the house which, with dark-stained wainscoting and more sombre furnishings, retains the long-influential atmosphere of its Victorian years.

One alteration was made to the villa by John Paris and that was the insertion of a bathroom. This was achieved by creating a landing halfway up the staircase and projecting it, along with additional cupboard room, out to the back and thus avoiding any interference with the aspect of the building from the front and sides. It is quite surprising to discover that here was a house that in the 1920s was still without those facilities which by then were usually taken for granted in most well maintained dwellinghouses. An old-fashioned bathtub, kept in a large closet later used as a china cupboard, was carried out, placed in front of the fire and filled with water from jugs and kettles.

Outside on the lawn are two ornamental summer-houses in the trees' shade, one of which was the tiny wooden 'laboratory' where John Paris conducted experiments in chemistry, and at the side of the house facing the evening sun was the greenhouse with its bright rows of plants and flowers.

The present owner of Strathavon Lodge had the unusual experience of delivering the Queen's telegram to Mr Paris on his 100th birthday in January 1979, when the weather during that severe winter was at its worst. Determined to get through the snow to Woodville, only a very short distance away, if, as she put it, she had to crawl on her hands and knees, she went out at the same moment that the driver of the mail van drew up outside and asked her to direct him. He had come too far, she said, and enquired if he would take her along with him in the van. He agreed to do so, and when she got out at the gate he handed her the last delivery of mail for Woodville for the day. Miss Hunter greeted her at the door: 'Come and see all the cards and flowers and telegrams — but there isn't one from the Palace'. 'Oh yes, there is,' she replied, 'and I have been given the privilege of bringing it!'

John Paris died in November 1979, two months before his 101st birthday. He was related to the Burrell family of Glasgow, one member of which, Sir William, achieved lasting fame as the creator of the renowned Burrell Collection of works of art of international repute which had to wait many years before a suitable home could be found for their permanent display to the public. John Paris's life at Woodville was in part a sad and lonely one. It was to this house that he brought his bride about the mid-1920s, not doubting it would be the family home for many years to come, only to lose her and their stillborn child in the first few years of marriage. The garden, with its evocative 'oldness' and individuality of atmosphere which leaves its impression on the visitor, became her memorial instead for over half a century.

Happily, Woodville is again in family ownership and further alterations, including the extension of the upper floor across the rest of the house, have been made. But memories of the past, and the recent past, still linger. Here, in the fragrant quietness, as you sat taking tea with Mr Paris and Miss Hunter on the grass beside the rosebeds, the Victorian flats, briefly visible on the south when the green depth of foliage stirred and lifted, and the much more recent houses in Laverockbank Road before it slopes steeply down towards the sea, seemed to fade strangely in the afternoon sun, while the shadows lengthened in the dark lime avenue, a rustle of silk became faintly audible above the rustle of leaves, and the long, high-waisted skirts of the Regency came gliding towards you momentarily through the trees.

CHAPTER 4

The House of Bangholm Bower

NOTWITHSTANDING the much older stone construction of a central block with two lower wings, in a short modern street on the southern edge of Trinity, not many people are aware today that the house of Bangholm Bower still stands where it did. This is partly due to its having been incorporated, shortly before the Second World War, into a double row of little villas then being built on the last stretch of ground belonging

Fig. 22.   Bangholm Bower, a house that has shed its broad acres since it was built in the early 19th century to become part of a street.

to the house to be disposed of, but even more to its having turned its back in silent resignation on the street, no doubt in nostalgia for its more spacious past, to face its graceful Georgian entrance and white-astragaled fanlight towards a carefully tended little flower garden bounded by a narrow rear lane.

The history of Bangholm Bower began when it was built as one of the 'principal mansions' in the area, as James Grant puts it in *Old and New Edinburgh*, not far from the old road which led to Trinity 'between hedgerows and trees' before 'the roads to Queensferry and Granton were constructed'. With its flanking pavilions and straightforward, symmetrical design, it is a typical example of the locally built early nineteenth-century Trinity villa.

Gradually, over many years, the lands of Bangholm Bower have been sold off in odd lots, large bits and small pieces. The dismantling process can be traced in detail only after it had shrunk to one acre and thirty falls lying to the west and two roods, three falls and thirty-five ells bounded by the road from Leith westward on the south, the first title deed thereafter being dated 1802. In 1812 there was a disposition in favour of the Merchant Company of Edinburgh and they, in turn, sold a large area of ground in 1872 to a Mr Houston Mitchell. From him it passed to the Maxwell family a few years later with whom it remained for two generations. The second Maxwell widow, Mrs Miller Maxwell, disponed a half of Bangholm Bower next to the Caledonian Railway to the Town Council of Edinburgh together with a further 117 square yards at the corner of Ferry Road and Trinity Road, the latter afterwards forming the Scout Field in South Trinity Road.

The property was again sold in 1926 for £3000, and it was about this time that the house itself was altered and subdivided into three separate units, a central three-storeyed house flanked by two smaller ones in each of the wings with tree-planted gardens to the front and back. The remaining ground was feued for housing and the final street development, which put an end to Bangholm Bower's long life as a free-standing mansionhouse, was completed shortly afterwards. On a map of Edinburgh published in the 1920s an area of approximately a quarter of a mile to the north of Ferry Road is designated 'Bangholm', and Bangholm Nursery is shown on both sides of the southern end of Clark Road. The north side of the new street spread bricks and mortar across the former rose garden, the site, if an old tradition can be relied upon, of the last duel to be fought in Edinburgh. Unfortunately the tradition does not include a date.

The large central house, while its street-numbered gate presents an uncompromising exterior anonymity to the passer-by, yet preserves in the much altered interior many interesting features from the past. The original back door has been elevated to front-entrance status and above it, lighting the curving wrought-iron staircase, is a tall, slender, round-headed window in painted glass which is typical of the period. Designs vary from house to house and this one, framed in an outer border of thistle, rose and shamrock motifs, contains four roundels, one above the other, depicting the seasons. In the first circle at the top, snowdrops represent the Spring, then, underneath, Summer contributes roses and a lily, followed below by the ripened fruits of Autumn, and finally a bush of holly symbolising Winter concludes the series at the foot.

On the first floor the now curtailed dimensions of the drawing-room happily retain, converted to electricity, four gas-light brackets, projecting from the walls on adjustable brass scrolls, three of them still having the pink glass globes which were bought for them about 1930, the only broken one being irreplaceable. The entrance hall and staircase ceilings are enriched with plasterwork of Adamesque design, and the rooms have similar frieze and cornice decoration. A white marble mantelpiece in the drawing-room contrasts attractively with rose pink fireplace tiles, also dating from the conversion, and another in one of the bedrooms, painted white, is decorated in the Adam manner with arabesque mouldings on either side of a jardinière containing grapes and vineleaves. A false door in the drawing-room formerly led to a still-room which is now part of one of the two houses in the separated wings.

Exploration uncovers a fascinating layout of narrow corridors which lead round, through other rooms and landings, to the original starting point. Liable to trip up the unwary, there is a sudden step down to a lower level where a modern kitchen and bathroom have been added to the house, and a narrow, wooden access, easily mistaken for a cupboard door (another feature typical of its time), opens unexpectedly on a secondary brass-railed staircase leading upwards, past a vast water cistern stretching far back into the shadows behind the wood panelling, to the attic floor. Here, at the top of the old mansion and in one of the two large dormer-windowed bedrooms, the house reserves one of its finest treasures, an incomparable view southwards to the Castle, the skyline of the Old Town and Princes Street and, if one leans out of the window on a day when visibility is good, to the Bass Rock and Berwick Law on the distant coastline.

Since its sub-division, the central house has had two unusual experiences. The first was on the day of the Queen's wedding, an event which no doubt helped to impress it on the memory of the mother and daughter who bought the house immediately after the conversion. (The daughter, a descendant of the Logans of Restalrig, of whom more later, died there, aged over ninety, in 1984). It may perhaps be remembered that Edinburgh was at that time suffering from an outbreak of what was then called 'weeping walls' due to rapid fluctuations in the temperature that summer, and the staircase walls of Bangholm Bower appeared to run copiously with blood! The cause was the quick condensation of the red paint (the famous red ochre, so universally used in the nineteenth century) with which they had been decorated years before. No less alarming was the second dilemma — the discovery one morning of bulging ceiling plaster above the staircase and the possibility, as they believed, of a cascade of water descending through the house. Water was not the gremlin in the situation this time, however, but, much more unexpectedly, air pressure, the pressure having built up against the plaster after an application of paint with an unsuitable chemical constituent, and the remedy was simple and permanent — its removal and replacement with distemper.

Today Bangholm Bower, having shed its acres gradually in roods and ells, and no longer sheltered and secluded by its ancient walls, stands in the contemplative dignity of age beside the neighbouring suburban villas, a stone's throw from the busy cross-road shoppers and the Leith-bound traffic.

St. Serf's Church was built on the site of Bangholm Farm, and the playing fields of George Heriot's School, entered from Inverleith Row, were once the fields belonging to the Farm.

CHAPTER 5

Three Roads to Leith

BY an odd historical coincidence, the origin of Leith Walk as the principal thoroughfare between Edinburgh and its Port can be attributed to the military strategy of an Englishman, none other than Oliver Cromwell himself, the only person ever to have deprived the country of a monarch. Angry at Scotland for proclaiming Charles II as its King and riding north to do battle with the Scots, he chose to threaten the capital by advancing towards it from the Port. In his *Traditions of Edinburgh* Robert Chambers describes what happened: 'At the approach of Cromwell to Edinburgh, immediately before the battle of Dunbar, Leslie, the Covenanting general, arranged the Scottish troops in a line, the right wing of which rested upon the Calton Hill, and the left upon Leith, being designed for the defence of these towns. A battery was erected at each extremity, and the line was itself defended by a trench and a mound, the latter composed of the earth dug from the former. Leslie himself took up his headquarters at Broughton, whence some of his despatches are dated. When the war was shifted to another quarter, this mound became a footway between the two towns'. Cromwell having been thwarted on Leith Walk (though not at Dunbar), the way was now clear for Charles, who regally rode along it from the Kirkgate into Edinburgh after being crowned at Scone.

During the following century, in 1748, Leith Walk, or Leith Loan as it was called originally, was described as a 'handsome gravel walk, twenty feet broad, which is kept in good repair at the public charge, and no horses suffered to come upon it'. In the course of time a second footpath was made at the bottom of the rampart, eighteen feet below the one on top, and to avoid confusion they were known as the High Walk and the Low Walk. A surviving example of the latter can still be seen at Springfield Cottage which stands at the foot of a flight of steps. A wooden paling prevents unwary walkers from falling down to the lower level. The street was left in this pedestrianised condition until 1769 when the new North Bridge was built to link the Old Town of Edinburgh with the open fields to the north upon which Princes Street and the New Town were eventually to spread out. As there was considerable opposition to this extension of the city boundaries, however, it was deemed advisable to suppress this information, and it was publicly announced that the new bridge was intended to facilitate communication between the City and the Port.

As a result of this new level access, the journey to Leith could now be made conveniently by horse and carriage, and the gravel surface of the Walk was soon churned into dust and pounded into pot-holes by the wheels and horses' hooves. This situation was tolerated, surprisingly, till the beginning of the nineteenth century when a 'splendid causeway was formed at a great expense by the city of Edinburgh, and a toll erected for its payment'.

Chambers recalls the Gallow Lee, a grim reminder of those bygone days when the country administered a stern public justice as rough, in many cases, as its unkept roads. 'One terrible peculiarity attended Leith Walk in its former condition. It was overhung by a gibbet, from which were suspended all culprits whose bodies at condemnation were sentenced to be hung in chains.' The ground on which it stood, adjacent to Shrub Hill, contained large quantities of sand, and the soil, enriched with the bones of centuries of malefactors, was sold by a speculating proprietor to be converted into mortar for the New Town houses!

Leith Walk in the early nineteenth century was a scene of 'enjoyments peculiarly devoted to children', and 'even the half-penniless boy might here get his appetite for wonders' gratified. In addition to caravan-shows, street singers and organ-grinders, few who had seen it as children ever forgot the waxworks 'which occupied a laigh shop opposite to the present Haddington Place'. The doorway of this entertaining establishment was decorated with parrots and birds of Paradise and a diminutive wax gentleman in the outmoded dress of a French courtier of the previous century who sat 'reading one eternal copy of the *Edinburgh Advertiser*'.

Leith Walk is described in an Edinburgh guidebook of about 1919 as having, some fifty or sixty years previously, been 'bounded on each side by nurseries, but [it] is now one continuous line of houses and shops, so that there is now no actual division between the two towns', the junction being at Pilrig.

It was in Leith Walk, in June 1821, that Thomas Carlyle, then living in Moray Street (subsequently Spey Street) near Pilrig, experienced the 'sudden spiritual awakening' which he afterwards transferred to his philosophic Germanic hero in *Sartor Resartus*. Carlyle re-enacts in the Rue St. Thomas de l'Enfer in Paris the salutary change in his attitude to life which he himself had met with in Leith Walk. He remembered the very spot where it occurred, 'just below Pilrig Street', as Professor Masson has recorded in his essay on Carlyle's Edinburgh life, while 'on his way to Leith'. As this incident happened immediately after his first meeting with Jane Welsh, whom he later married, the two events are probably not unconnected!

In the later nineteenth century Leith Walk seems to have become a sadly neglected thoroughfare. In a cri de coeur to the *Leith Burghs Pilot* in 1866, a correspondent complains of a lack of conveniences of more kinds than one, including drinking fountains and seats on which to 'rest and be thankful'. He deplores the unrepaired condition of the street which in wet weather 'represents a series of miniature fish ponds' and would 'disgrace a third class fishing village'. The Town Council, he says cynically, should 'mend their ways' in the 'Leith division of the Walk'.

Street names in this area often commemorate people who lived or had their business premises there. Thus the quaint, curving little side street known as Stead's Place recalls Mr

Fig. 23. Middlefield, a Georgian country house surviving behind Leith Walk.

Stead and his card factory (which made combs for carding wool), and at the end of Smith's Place, facing the Walk, the elegant and classical but now commercialised mansion called Smith's Place, built in 1812, has ensured that its owner's name would be given to the street. Behind the Walk on the other side, at Shrub Place, survives the Georgian country house of Middlefield (no doubt so named in reference to its original surroundings), the straight-line of the street going along in front of it. Built in 1796, this attractive building, with a pilastered doorway beneath a pedimented central window flanked by two Venetian windows, and crowned with a gabled attic storey, deserves to be made more of and restored.

Fig. 24.   Bonnington Village, now being reorientated to the 20th century behind Newhaven Road.

Mr Anderson's Iron Foundry was on the other side of his garden wall and, with the exception of a few houses on the east side at the foot of the wide thoroughfare to Leith, the ground here was mainly open and undeveloped.

Before the completion of Leith Walk the two principal routes to Leith were Bonnington Road on the west and, as its name implies, Easter Road from the opposite direction. The area around the London Road end of the latter has been connected with the name of Norton since the second half of the eighteenth century, the association beginning when the Hon. Fletcher Norton, son of Lord Grantley of Yorkshire and Attorney General in England, came to Scotland after the

Fig. 25. Bonnington Mill, long disused and now demolished.

unsuccessful Jacobite Rebellion of 1745. He was appointed a Baron of the Scottish Exchequer in 1776 and took up residence in a house, long since demolished, which stood on the site of Abbeyhill Station. Winning the confidence and respect of the people as a Judge, he soon overcame the prejudice and suspicion which still prevailed against the English. With his Scottish wife and family, he lived at Abbeyhill until his death in 1820, and his name is still commemorated in Norton Place and in a single surviving dwellinghouse now curiously situated in a drying green behind Easter Road. This is Norton Villa and, although still, happily, occupied as a family home, it is completely screened

Fig. 26. Bonnington Mill House, badly deteriorated and not likely to survive.

from view by the shops and tenements of one of the busiest streets in the district. Bay windows on both floors on one side, and a barge-boarded porch outside the entrance in the centre, give a Victorian appearance to this little, reputedly eighteenth-century, building.

Bonnington Road has witnessed the thriving life of its village by the Water of Leith where the earliest woollen manufacturers in Scotland lived and traded, and, when the *Great Michael* was launched in 1504, James IV, grandfather of Mary Queen of Scots, rode across its bridge in a Royal progress to that other port of Newhaven which he had vainly hoped would outstrip Leith in nautical pre-eminence. Today the road will lead you past the substantial remnants of the old Bonnington Village without even hinting at its presence, but you can diverge at Rosebank Cemetery, opened on the corner of Bonnington Road and Pilrig Street in 1846, and follow the lane at the back of Newhaven Road for a few hundred yards. Here the old viaduct that used to carry the little branch line noisily above the crossroads has been cut off and rises, sullen and foreshortened, behind the village, until recently a derelict, unexpected, survival, like an unpropitious signpost to the future. Backing on to Newhaven Road itself was the disused and disconsolate mill, with the gaunt and empty Mill House adjoining at right angles, a makeshift outside stair indicating that it had once been subdivided to house two families. A few years ago permission was obtained by a builder to create modern residential accommodation within the old village buildings which it was agreed should be retained although the Mill House has deteriorated to such an extent that it will probably have to be demolished. It is highly unfortunate that, by waiting for two years and resubmitting similar plans to those which were initially rejected, the builder was allowed to demolish the mill for the purpose of making another access from Newhaven Road, and one more irreplaceable historical asset has thus been lost to the city.

Beyond, and nearer the stream from which a mill-lade once bore its waterpower to turn the wheel, is a row of cottages, and in front, looking towards the abruptly halted stride of the railway arches, is the old mansion of Bonnyhaugh, a three-storeyed, rubble-built house erected in 1621 by the Town Council of Edinburgh, who had purchased the mills four years previously, for a Dutch dyer called Jeromias van der Heill whom they had brought over from Holland to teach the craft in Edinburgh. About 1713 it became the 'secluded villa' of Bishop Robert Keith, scholar, historian and churchman. His *Catalogue of Scottish Bishops* was a valuable work of reference of the Scottish Episcopal Church, and the list of subscribers to his *History of the Church and State of Scotland* read, says Chambers, like a 'muster roll of the whole Jacobite

Fig. 27. The house of Bonnyhaugh, the home of Bishop Keith at the time of the Jacobite Risings and now converted into flats.

nobility'. Bishop Keith corresponded with Prince Charles Edward Stuart in France, but on the subject of ecclesiastical rather than political affairs. Having ministered conscientiously to his small Episcopal communion for many years, he died in Bonnyhaugh in 1757 and was buried, deeply mourned by them, in the Canongate Churchyard. The interior of Bonnyhaugh is now being altered to provide a dwellinghouse and two flats.

From Bonnington Toll down to the old mill Newhaven Road is bounded by the garden wall of the strange little mansion of Stewartfield — a high structure with a massive chimney stack crowning its steeply pitched roof — the casting down of which has to be laid at the door of a previous generation.

Still standing in Ferry Road, but architecturally different from the rest of it, is Bonnington Bank House with its little forecourt garden and larger one behind. It is adjoined by the lower addition which in recent years has been converted into the Coach House Theatre. This late Georgian building with Victorian extensions was the Town House of the Earls of Mar and Kellie and is now owned by the Roman Catholic Church and used as a Laity Centre.

These highways of ancient origin are still the roads that lead to Leith, but they can now be traversed with rather more rapidity than could be achieved by those who were carried thither by the stage coach around two hundred years ago; it 'took an hour and a half to go from the Tron Church to the Shore', and was 'a great lumbering affair on four wheels, the two fore painted yellow, the two hind red, having formerly belonged to different vehicles', and was drawn by a pair of 'ill-conditioned, ill-sized hacks'. Today the traffic faces other and acuter problems, change follows frequent change upon the face of Leith, and few people would now recognise either an old description of the Walk, that former rampart of defence against the invading Roundheads (whose battle on the site of Leith Links with its defenders was re-enacted in 1983 by the Sealed Knot Society as part of the 500th anniversary celebrations of South Leith Church), or the gastronomic rewards after its leisurely perambulation. It was, wrote John Geddie, 'the favourite "walk" of citizens, old and young, on their way to enjoy the fresh salt breezes on Leith pier and to put an edge on appetites that could afterwards be blunted by feasting on the succulent "Pandore oysters", for which the Old Ship Inn and other taverns on the Shore were famed'.

CHAPTER 6

The Port and the Crown

'THE cannon-shots from the galleys, as they contrived to near Leith harbour, were, doubtless, a sufficient advertisement. Soon, so far as the fog would permit, all Leith was in proper bustle, and all the political and civic dignitaries that chanced to be in Edinburgh were streaming to Leith.' Thus did David Masson, Professor of English Literature in the University of Edinburgh at the end of the nineteenth century, describes, three hundred years after the event, the arrival in Scotland of Mary, Queen of Scots, after thirteen years at the French court to enter fully and inexorably into her inheritance of a crown, a throne and a turbulent and troubled country. The day, wrote John Knox, who might be expected to remember it, was so dark and 'the myst so thick' that 'skairse mycht any man espy ane other the length of two pair of butts'. Mary had set sail from Calais on 14th August 1561, two French galleys and other ships conveying the Queen, representatives of the French nobility and their 'rich and splendid baggage' towards the fog-bound Scottish coast.

When she had stepped ashore 'she took some rest', says Professor Masson, 'in the house in Leith deemed most suitable for her reception, the owner being Andrew Lamb, a wealthy Leith merchant', a house which, though altered, is well known in the Port to the present time. It is probable that Mary herself often looked back to that day of mirk and mist, so typical of her capital and its seaport but also so prophetic of the clouds that were soon to cast their shadows on her uneasy reign. She was not the first of Scotland's queens to land at Leith, or to have had cause to lament 'the surfett weat and corruptioun of the air', as Knox expressed it. Her father, James V, before his second marriage to Mary of Guise, the mother of the Queen of Scots who had succeeded to the throne when just a few days old, had wedded the beautiful

Fig. 28.   Lamb's House, where Mary Queen of Scots rested on her return to Scotland in 1561, and now probably the best known building in Leith where it serves as an Old People's Day Centre.

but delicate Magdalene, daughter of Francis I of France, who died only eight weeks after stooping down to kiss the soil of Scotland at disembarkation in her husband's kingdom.

To the earlier Mary, daughter of the Duke of Guise, Leith was to become much more than a landing stage en route to Edinburgh Castle. It was her misfortune, wrote Chambers in the *Traditions of Edinburgh*, 'to be placed in a position to resist the Reformation. Her own character deserved that she should have stood in a more agreeable relation to what Scotland now venerates, for she was mild and just, and sincerely anxious for the welfare of her adopted country'. Like her daughter, she would not abandon the ancient faith of France, and her last outpost before defeat was the Port of Leith. Though by then she was ill and, indeed, dying, it was well and stubbornly defended by the Queen Regent with strong support from the French who in June 1548, under the Scottish flag, sailed into the roads of Leith in twenty-two galleys and as many as six hundred other ships, if Calderwood's account is accurate. The besieged were frequently the attackers in this bitter struggle, and the English Army, which reinforced the 'raw levies' of the Lords of the Congregation, won no quick or even outright victory against Mary and the French who made several sallies outside their own fortifications when battle between the opposing sides was joined with 'sword and pike' on the Links of Leith.

Little evidence is left of these old wars today except on the Links themselves where the English raised two mounds armed with guns, 250 yards apart, known as Pelham's Battery and Somerset's Battery after the English officers in charge of them. Cannon were also placed on the tower of St. Anthony's Preceptory which has vanished from the scene as well. The townspeople of the Port were not slow to change the martial nomenclature of the mounds, which were eventually taken over as adventure playgrounds by their children who, finding it a steeper climb, called the larger of them Giant's Brae. The other was dubbed Lady Fife's Brae after the Countess of Fife who lived immediately southwards of the mound in Hermitage House. Cannonballs fired into the 'Kirk of Leith' from Somerset's Battery (Giant's Brae) on 15th April 1560 are preserved in the entrance vestibule of South Leith Church. Writing in the 1880s, Grant adds a pleasant, peaceful footnote to the history of these mounds. 'When the young grass is sprouting in Spring,' he writes, 'the zig-zags that led there-from to the walls can often be distinctly traced in the Links.'

But the Queen Regent did not live to see the end. She considered the possibility of her return to France and the appointment of a new French Regent in her place. She even attempted to sue for peace with England. But on 10th June

1560, the year that saw the establishment of the Reformed Church in Scotland, she died, while waiting anxiously for news from the town of Leith, in Edinburgh Castle.

Her daughter, widowed by the death of her French husband, condemned herself to certain sorrow when she married Henry Darnley, and it is pleasant to read of an act of charity done jointly by them both during their short married life. Having been petitioned to do so, they granted power to the skippers of Leith, for the better ordering of navigation, to 'take tryall' of all seamen and apprentices before allowing them to sail, and to apply the fees, and the fines imposed on those found wanting, to support the poor.

When Mary left Scotland for the last time she did not go by sea, but on horseback and in a hurry and without a crown.

If the seagate to Edinburgh meant entrances to dool and skaith to his mother and grandmother, James VI took with him happier memories of the Port to his English inheritance when he added that other and much more coveted crown of the southern kingdom to his regalia. It was from here that he set out, in October 1589, to claim Anne of Denmark, who had been frustrated by westerly gales in her journey towards Scotland, as his bride. More fearless in the face of potential danger than he often showed himself, James braved the hazards of the waning year and sailed, like the saintly Brandan, to the northern main. The marriage ceremony, performed by The Rev. David Lindsay of South Leith Church, took place in Norway where Anne was stormbound, almost as soon as he set foot on land.

The King and Queen then spent some months in Denmark before setting forth for Leith in the April or early May of 1590. James, who would not return to Scotland without a Scottish pilot ship, had sent off a message to the Provost and Town Council of Edinburgh requiring them to find and furnish one to fetch him home. They discovered a vessel, bound for Elsinore, was about to leave Kirkcaldy. She was called the *Ayngell*, and the safety of Their Majesties was entrusted to her experienced crew. These precautions

Fig. 29. The King's Wark, used for many purposes by the Stewart Kings and now one of the principal ancient monuments of Leith.

notwithstanding, this Spring crossing was attended by more alarms and excursions at sea than the outward voyage had been in the later season. James firmly believed that the 'incantations of witches' had been the cause of his rough passage and, although no harm had come to the Royal barque, another vessel bearing gifts for the Queen was sent to the bottom between Burntisland and the Port.

Disembarking on the Shore at Leith, James and his bride were welcomed by the firing of cannon and the discharging of an equally sonorous loyal address in Latin, after which they proceeded to the King's Wark where all was in readiness for their reception. When the coronation procession arrived in the ancient capital of his race, James rode on horseback, the

Queen followed in a regal chariot, and the gutters of the Auld Toun ran red with wine for the rude populace from the Mercat Cross.

Charles II, great-grandson of the Queen of Scots, had less pleasant memories of Scotland than had James VI, his grandfather. Proclaimed King in 1649 at the Mercat Cross of Edinburgh (no flowing fount of Bacchus on this occasion) at the age of 18 and a week after the execution of Charles I, he was invested with his right to the crown of Scotland but not yet that of England, which country was to be ruled by the Parliamentarians for the next ten years. The Scottish crown had been forfeited by his father because he refused to accept the Solemn League and Covenant, and the younger Charles had to make up his mind about the same burning question. It was soon clear to him that, if he wanted to take the crown, he would have to take the Covenant as well, so he allied himself to a cause which he liked, in fact, no better than Charles I had done. This arrangement was unwelcome news in the South, and Cromwell decided to persuade the Scots by force of arms to give up their King. Yet again a warlike host marched northwards but David Leslie, the commander of the Scottish Army, had no intention of allowing the Roundheads to get into Leith, as this would give them control of the harbour in which their ships carrying the ever necessary provisions could have anchored safely. As mentioned in the previous chapter, the victory in this encounter went to the Scots. In the meantime Charles, after his entertainment at a banquet in the Parliament House in Edinburgh in July 1650, 'thairafter went down to Leith to ane ludging belonging to the Lord Balmerinoch' which was placed at his disposal 'during his abyding in Leith'.

The King received the Scottish crown from the Marquis of Argyle at Scone in January 1651, but Leslie's army, after several reverses, was finally defeated at the Battle of Worcester in the following Autumn and Leslie himself was taken prisoner. Charles fled abroad, and nine years were to elapse before the Restoration of the Monarchy in England

made it possible for him to return. With the crown he most
wanted now firmly on his head, he instructed Sir William
Bruce, his Architect in Scotland, to enlarge and embellish his
Palace of Holyroodhouse in Edinburgh but, scunnered at
Scotland by the psalm and the conventicle, he did not come
back to see or live in it. Nor did any of his successors for over
one hundred and fifty years, and the crown itself lay hidden
in a chest in Edinburgh Castle.

If Mary, Queen of Scots, could dimly have foreseen the
future, as perhaps she tried to do from time to time within the
prison walls that closed around her so early in her stressful
life, it is not impossible that she presaged a prolongation of
the Stuart line, and the crown, even the longed-for crown of a
United Kingdom, being inherited by her heirs, but it is hardly
probable that she could have conjured up the scene at Leith
when, the direct line from Mary having been rejected, an
alien German Prince stood upon the Shore to receive a
rapturous greeting from the descendants of her subjects.
Scotland had to await the advent of Sir Walter Scott to bring
the King to its capital and rescue the crown from its
concealment.

On 15th August 1822 King George IV, on board the *Royal
George*, arrived with escorting frigates in the Roads of Leith
'and a salute from the battery announced that all had come to
anchor'. Sir Walter was among the first on board to welcome
him and was not above putting a souvenir of the occasion in
his pocket, a glass from which the former Prince Regent had
drunk being conveniently to hand. In his absorption in the
proceedings, however, he absentmindedly sat down, and the
glass was crushed to fragments.

A barge brought the King ashore, watched admiringly by
probably the largest crowd the Port had ever witnessed whose
'acclamations', being 'all unused to royalty, seemed to rend
heaven'. To this tumult of sound was added the firing of
ships' cannon and the skirling of pipers on the pier, while 'the
combined cheers of the mighty multitude filled up the pauses'.
As well he might be, George IV was 'visibly affected' by his

Fig. 30. The Shore, Leith, from the Victoria Swing Bridge at Leith Docks.
It was here that George IV landed on his famous visit to Scotland in 1822.
The Signal Tower is on the left.

reception, and the success of his one and only State visit to
Scotland turned out to be a salutary influence on the manner
in which he addressed himself to the art of kingship on his
return to London. Never a memorable monarch, he was a
slightly more significant one after experiencing such unearned
and unexpected Scottish loyalty. George IV's disembarkation
at The Shore was depicted on the one-guinea note issued by
the Leith Banking Company, with the Customs House in
Commercial Street designed by Robert Reid in 1812 in the
background. The Bank was founded in 1793 and ceased
trading in 1842. Each note recorded the Banking Company's
promise 'to pay the bearer one pound one shilling on demand
at their office in Leith'.

From the ramparts of Edinburgh Castle the King looked out
over the new-built houses of the partially completed New

Town, the waters of the Forth and the distant hills, and confessed he had not known that such a view existed in his kingdom. But Leith was not to see him again. After a final glittering occasion in his honour at Hopetoun House, he rejoined the *Royal George* at Port Edgar, and sailed for home.

These had been very different scenes from sad Mary's homecoming to the pier at Leith, when Knox had never seen so dolorous a face of heaven, but it is the enigma that was Mary that has exercised the minds and imaginations of every succeeding generation, for the crown never rested on a more tragic or a more romantic head.

CHAPTER 7
The Port and the Town

THE troubles of Leith, frequently lamented by its historians, are of ancient origin, and the blame has been laid squarely at the door of the sister city where, unfortunately, it undoubtedly belongs. They began, presumably unintentionally, in the early years of the fourteenth century when King Robert the Bruce forged the first link in its chain of servitude by making a grant of the Port to the burgesses of Edinburgh, who, apparently not satisfied with that substantial acquisition, went on to obtain control of the harbour in addition which they administered, in the interests of Edinburgh, for five hundred years.

The Bruce charter did not include any right to the banks of the Water of Leith, then, as already mentioned, a larger and deeper waterway than it has since become, and disputes with Sir Robert Logan, to whom they belonged, were not infrequent. The actual superiority of Leith was in the hereditary possession of the Logans of Restalrig, a family which played an intermittent and, particularly in the case of the last baron in the long line of Robert Logans at the end of the sixteenth century, a plotting, scheming role behind the scenes in Scottish history, and whose race stretched back to very early times. Towards the end of the fourteenth century a Robert Logan married into the family of Lestalric, thus acquiring Leith as well as the barony later known as Restalrig, and their son married a daughter of Robert II. For many generations Leith was held in fee by their successors, who exacerbated the plight of the Port by selling out to Edinburgh in 1398 under a bond described as 'exclusive, ruinous and enslaving' in terms of which wharfs and quays were to be built along the river banks, granaries and shops erected and roads constructed to meet the growing need for better transport. Taken at its face value, this might have been

considered an enlightened civic policy of investment in the
future prosperity of Leith, but such a desirable result was far
from being the outcome or, for that matter, the intention.
Trade was unquestionably to be increased (from the sixteenth
century onwards more foreign ships put into Leith than any
other port in Scotland) and business to flourish but, owing to
punitive preconditions dictated by the Town, the profits went
not to the Port which was earning them but to the Capital.

For the diversion of revenues from Leith there were several
explanations. The magistrates and Town Council of
Edinburgh gradually obtained the superiority of the whole of
Leith, the only exceptions being Yardheads, which takes its
name from the walls bounding the orchards belonging to the
Canons of St. Anthony's, and the lands of St. Anthony's
themselves; for them the dues were paid to the Kirk Session of
South Leith Church. The old Preceptory of the Canons had
been founded about 1430, approximately fifty years earlier
than the church dedicated to St. Mary. The Preceptory,
which was sited close to St. Mary's, owed its existence to the
Logans of Restalrig and there, in accordance with custom and
their own instructions, they were to be 'prayit for ilk Sunday
till the day of doom'. About thirty years after the
Reformation, by which time the last of the remaining monks
had probably died, the monastic funds were made over to St.
Mary's, which by that time was known as South Leith
Church. It had been the only foundation of the Order of St.
Anthony in Scotland.

The ancient Church of St. Mary's stood in the Kirkgate
opposite the Trinity House which was built by the Masters
and Mariners of Leith and rebuilt in a classical style with
central pediment and groups of twin columns in 1816 by the
architect Thomas Brown. St. Mary's was not the earliest place
of worship for the people of South Leith, as Restalrig was
then the predominant town with its own church serving the
whole area, and it was for the purpose of providing a church
in the immediate locality that the Kirkgate site was chosen for
the new foundation in the late fifteenth century. As it was

dedicated to the Virgin, she was adopted as the patron saint of the Port, and the Madonna and Child within a canopied galley then became incorporated in the Arms of Leith. Restalrig Church itself was desecrated during the Reformation and was only rebuilt in 1838, by William Burn, with a few fragments of the original choir still surviving. The adjoining St. Triduana's Well, also now restored, was a place of pilgrimage for those suffering from diseases of the eyes, the spring of remedial water being enclosed by a vaulted chapel with a central column which has the appearance of a mediaeval chapter-house.

The trade incorporations had their chapels, which they maintained at their own expense, in St. Mary's, and a lamp hung over the statue of Our Lady above the high altar.

Trinity House and St. Mary's, rebuilt in 1848 by Thomas Hamilton and now the Parish Church of South Leith, with its burial ground, are almost the sole relics of a historic past in the heart of the old community, the Kirkgate having been badly mutilated in recent years. Another prominent but now vanished building in that ancient street was a tavern, or restaurant, known as Cant's Ordinary, mine host being Mr Cant, a member of a family then well known in Leith. Perhaps the best way of explaining the name of this quaint, archaic edifice with its arcaded frontage is to quote a few lines from James Boswell's *Life of Johnson*, where the word 'Ordinary' is used in the same connection: '. . . happening to dine at Clifton's eating house, in Butcher-row, I was surprised to perceive Johnson come in and take his seat at another table. The mode of dining, or rather being fed, at such houses in London is well known to many to be particularly unsocial, as there is no Ordinary, or united company, but each person has his own mess and is under no obligation to hold any intercourse with any one'.

The economic factors were also strongly slanted in Edinburgh's favour, Royal Burghs possessing a monopoly of trading rights over a much wider area than their own boundaries. As a result, no buying and selling could take place in Leith itself but only in the recognised Edinburgh markets and at prices laid down by the City. Marketable commodities could only be assessed and weighed within the Royal Burgh and stent, or tax, was payable on all such goods before they could be offered for sale. Infringement of such laws was not, of course, uncommon, with business being conducted outside the prescribed demarcations and merchandise being 'passed over garden walls' to avoid the dues.

No Leith trader could become a burgess, nor could he enter into partnership with an Edinburgh merchant, and no burgess was permitted to reside in Leith. Those who, by so doing, attempted to evade their responsibilities as 'freemen' while retaining and enjoying their privileges, went in danger of being removed from office. In the year 1580 a 'candil maker' called Thomas Lamb was 'callit and accuset for meltein of tallow in the unfrie toun of Leyth', and anyone discovered buying imported goods directly from the seller was fined for his audacity and had his ill-gotten purchases impounded, as they should first, according to the rules, have been bought by the magistrates and sent to the marketplace in Edinburgh.

The narrow thoroughfare known as Burgess Close was, as its name implied, out of bounds to the unfree men of Leith, and it was here that the counting-houses of the Edinburgh burgesses were located. Leith traders who wished to ship their wares to a foreign port had to pay the appropriate tariff and obtain a licence.

In early times the working life of Leithers was carried out under the aegis of four incorporations, the mariners, the brewers and maltmen, traders (such as coopers, cordiners, bakers and others), and the merchants and shopkeepers, their original charter having been granted by the Logans of Restalrig in the sixteenth century. The members of these incorporations, who could not of course be burgesses, could only protect their interests by erecting monopolies that were as jealously guarded as those of the craft guilds of Edinburgh. This state of affairs was not remedied until 1734 when, by a declaration of their independence from the Town, the Leith traders were no longer referred to as unfree. Each incorporation had originally established an altar to its patron saint in the parish church, and contributions were made by the members towards defraying the costs involved as well as to a much-needed fund for relieving the poor and the infirm.

The Incorporation of Coopers of Leith made common cause with the Fleshers and Masons in upholding the altar of St. John in the New Kirk of Our Lady, and it was this church which, after many vicissitudes, became at last the Parish Church of South Leith. The Sederunt Books of the Coopers, as of other incorporations, are still extant. Their funds were built up by the ingathering of weekly dues from their craftsmen, and strangers taking up booths in the town for the exercise of the craft had to obtain permission to do so and to make payment of the dues and taxes exigible. Those who failed to provide meal for the chaplain were 'poinded' (i.e. had their property confiscated), and fines were imposed on any craftsmen who spoiled their work, which they had to 'mend' at their own expense. In the nineteenth century the Coopers' minute books recorded case after case of hardship and deprivation among their members, and the corporation's carefully considered and frequently reviewed attempts to mitigate them. When an application was received from a member, he was called before their elected representatives and examined as to whether he derived any pecuniary aid from other sources. If his need was deemed genuine, he might be granted such meagre assistance as '3/- per week but only until next quarter day', or if he were already in receipt of benefit to the extent of 6/- weekly, he ran the risk of having it reduced to five after a twelvemonth.

The Burlaw Court dealt with matters agricultural which were also of considerable importance to the life of Leith. Corn grew in the fields to landward of the Port, and rules were drawn up by the court to prevent abuses. A proclamation of 1710 prohibited the bringing in of corn after 7 o'clock in the evening after the discovery that it was being 'stollan and embezeled from the fields and brought into this toun under cloud of night'. The ground was sown to a large extent with pease, and pigs, sheep and geese were kept by the farming community. The Burlaw Court was empowered to fine anyone found 'lying doun amongst corn' or 'treading doun and pulling ye complainers pease or turkie beans'. The Court continued its functions until the middle of the eighteenth century and met on the south side of the Links at Duncat, or Dovecot, Yard, weather permitting. On inclement days it was held in Clephane's Tavern.

During the troubled period when Mary of Guise ruled as Queen Regent, she gave an undertaking to erect Leith into a Burgh of Barony as a preliminary to its being raised to the status of a Royal Burgh, and with this end in view she purchased the superiority from Sir Robert Logan for the benefit of the citizenry. This superiority included the Links and placed a still larger area of the Port under the authority of the Town when, to the continuing detriment of Leith, she died a few years after this enlightened step. Her daughter, Mary Queen of Scots, having less reason to show gratitude to the people of the Port, granted the superiority to the City. One advantage alone remained from these aborted plans. Leith was now reckoned as a town, having till then counted only as a village.

The few featureless back streets between Bernard Street and Tower Street and still known as Timber Bush are all that remain of the little mercantile enclave in Leith where, and where alone, the Town of Edinburgh countenanced the storing of goods unloaded at the quays. It has a colourful history that is as interestingly instructive about the bygone life of Leith as it is unexpected in so unpromising a place. The unusual name is a corruption of Timber Bourse which at once explains the nature of its use, for it was here that the timber merchants carried on their business which was probably considerable, bearing in mind the large amount of wood required by the wrights and builders and the famous Memel pine imported from the Baltic. This was no ordinary, run-of-the-mill set of commercial bargaining booths, however. Taking its inspiration, as usual, from the auld ally across the North Sea and, indeed, its name as well, it was a Merchants' Exchange quite in the Continental manner. A paved piazza with seats and benches was enclosed by stone arches supported on columns, and it is to be regretted that no trace of this remarkable early seventeenth-century edifice has survived. It was the brainchild of Bernard Lindsay, Gentleman of the Bedchamber to King James VI, whose name is commemorated in Bernard Street. From James, in 1606, he received that other notable pile, the King's Wark, within a dale's length of the Timber Bush, which happily still stands, restored and functioning, at the waterside. The generosity of the Wisest Fool in Christendom would not be over-estimated by those who knew that the favoured recipient had himself met the cost of making good the old structure which was then in need of repair. When he was at it the King's 'chalmer chiel', who had married Barbara, a daughter of the notorious Logans, in 1589, decided to make this the 'chief ornament' of Leith, and to enhance its environs he built the piazza and a tennis court on which James himself was pleased to demonstrate his skill during a visit to the Port in 1617. This property was conveyed to the Edinburgh Magistrates, and in 1649 the tennis court was reconstructed as a weigh-house.

An Admiralty Court was held in the Tolbooth but, losing its maritime functions by degrees, it became eventually a purely civic institution, although the titles of Admiral and Admirals Depute (in the seventeenth century the duties of the Admiral were carried out by the less pretentiously styled Water Bailie) were used by the Provost and Bailies after 1833 when, as a result of the Reform Act, Leith was granted the status of a Parliamentary Burgh. It had its own Town Council now and, by the passing of the Leith Act in 1827, Magistrates had been given permission to reside in Leith. In 1826 the Town's five hundred-year-old administration of the Harbour came to an end when it was handed over to the Dock Commissioners after another skirmish with the Edinburgh

Town Council. The Docks having become bankrupt, a proposal to sell them together with the Harbour to a joint stock company, the profits of which would be used to repay the dockland debts, seemed to offer a convenient solution. This was, however, one instance when the city failed in its exploitation of the Port and, in Lord Cockburn's words, 'fell into a pit dug by itself'. Some members of the Council were discovered to have bought shares for their own personal gain and, the trustees having therefore sold their own entrusted property to themselves, the whole scheme was summarily abandoned.

The Port had got its freedom from the Town at last. Its prosperity during these independent years was such that during the period 1871 to 1881 the population increased by more than 13,000. But its freedom was to be comparatively short-lived. With the extension of the Edinburgh boundaries in 1920 Leith was brought within the confines of the City, and its long-awaited and hard-won Town Council ceased to exist. During the period of its existence it was customary, on the appointment of a new burgess, for the Town Clerk to express the wish that he might never want the staff of life, in token of which he was then presented with a penny bap!

The decisive part played in the history of Leith by the Logans of Restalrig came to an abrupt end during the reign of James VI. The last baron, the then Sir Robert Logan, became a participant in that strange enigma in Scotland's annals known as the Gowrie Conspiracy. His part, as much surrounded by mystery as the other aspects of that extraordinary drama, was discovered after his death, and it was in macabre keeping with this curious episode that his bones were exhumed and put on trial in 1609. A sentence of forfeiture was passed on Logan's skeleton, but it is on record that this was reversed a few years afterwards. On the clifftop above Lochend Loch a fragment of his old fortified house or castle overhangs the water. Seen from the other side, it is less impressive, as an undistinguished extension was built on to it during the nineteenth century. It was here that the ultimate

Fig. 31.   Above the waters of Lochend Loch stands a fragment of the old stronghold of the Logans of Restalrig, Lochend House.

baron of the Logan line is said to have clung, as far as his diminished resources would allow, to the last vestiges of feudal pomp, while plotting secretly to out-plot the King who was secretly plotting to obtain the crown of England.

Cockburn's comments on the old and bitter feud between the Port and the Town were bluntly to the point. They had both been intemperate and unreasonable, he said, and 'if Leith had the advantage in coarse violence, Edinburgh was compensated by its superiority in disdainful insolence . . . The true value of the affair lay in its aiding the growth of independence in Leith'.

D

Fig. 32. John's Place, a delightful example of the short-lived Georgian development in Leith and for many years a favourite choice for foreign consulates in the Port.

The final chapter in the long and often unedifying Leith/Edinburgh saga has yet to be written, but there are many encouraging signs that some of the old life and vigour are returning to the Port, which can only augur well for the future of the ancient capital city as a whole.

CHAPTER 8

Pilrig House

A country residence between Edinburgh and Leith was for many years of its existence an accurate description of Pilrig House. But towns no more than time are prone to standing still, and the City and the Port gradually but inexorably strode out towards each other across the intervening fields and ultimately met at Pilrig, a convenient point of junction trafficwise till well into the twentieth century. Its future dependent on enlightened conservation in an increasingly inimical environment, conservation has lost out, and at the present time the house stands vandalised to an empty, gutted shell in a public park. Throughout a lifespan of almost three and a half centuries, a curious, colourful and, until a few years ago, continuous history can be traced between its rise and its ruin.

The name of Pilrig, originally Peelrig, is derived from an early peel tower which stood in the vicinity. In the sixteenth century these lands were in the hereditary possession of the family of Monypenny, lairds of Pilrig, one of whom, Robert, was killed on the battlefield of Pinkie in 1547 when that veteran intruder the Earl of Hertford, by then the Duke of Somerset and Protector of England, continued Henry VIII's attempts to destroy the Auld Alliance with the French and routed the ill-led Scottish Army beside the River Esk at Musselburgh. The Monypenny tenure came to an end in 1623 when Pilrig was acquired from them by Gilbert Kirkwood, a goldsmith, who built the house in 1638. For many years it remained a typical, sturdy, Scottish L-plan structure of the early seventeenth century in harled rubble and probably incorporated part of an earlier building on the same site. In the roof above the attic floor were dormer windows ornamented with finials carved as crescents and fleurs-de-lys, two bearing also the date of building. It being common

Fig. 33.   Pilrig House, built in 1638 and for long the home of the Balfours of Pilrig.

practice at this period to record, in addition to the date, the initials of the founder and his wife on the walls where they first set up house together, often in the attractive form of a 'marriage lintel' above the door, one of the window pediments was thus adorned at Pilrig when Gilbert Kirkwood married Margaret Foulis of Ravelston and established himself in the domestic style and comfort then available to a prosperous merchant and his family. Several of the rooms contained wood panelling which appears to be Memel pine, and this would certainly have accorded with contemporary trading patterns across the North Sea, timber being imported from the Baltic in exchange for Scottish coal and salt.

Tradition, however, asserts that it was cut down on the Burgh Muir, and that rough, virgin southern outskirt is known with certainty to have abounded in oaks which were used for the wooden projections of the 'timmer lands' that caused the narrow streets of the Old Town to become narrower by seven feet on either side. The influence of Dutch and Flemish architecture, so familiar to the Leith and other east-coast merchants who made the crossing frequently in the course of business, was reflected in the curving chimney gable in the centre of the south front, with a little circular window introduced as well. The classically columned doorway on this wall is probably of later date and was reached by a short flight of steps with an iron handrail.

The long association of Pilrig with the Balfour family began in 1718 when the property was bought by James Balfour, a merchant in Leith, who styled himself 'of Pilrig'. It was the fourth Balfour of Pilrig who, in 1828, made the extensive alterations to the house that gave it the external appearance which it retained for the rest of its active life, its latter years being devoted to such a variety of purposes as would have surprised, and eventually, when no further purposes could be contrived, greatly saddened its earlier owners. Balfour employed William Burn, an architect much in demand during the early nineteenth century and probably best known today for his detrimental 'over-restoration' of St. Giles, to fill in the angle of the 'L' in the original plan. This partially destroyed the older vernacular style, but besides increasing the accommodation it gave the Balfours, as they no doubt intended, a more modern and 'prestigious' mansionhouse.

Balfour Street, leading from Leith Walk down to the present Pilrig Park, was called after the proprietors of the estate and was originally an avenue of stately trees that 'opened westward from the Walk to the old Manor House' but was apparently never used as a means of access. The whins, heather and straw on the Pilrig policies, however, had proved more serviceable when, in remoter times, they were given by the lady of Pilrig House to be burned as a primitive disinfectant in the many unfortunate homes that were visited by the plague during outbreaks in the city, when all such dwellings were 'purgeit and cleansit with fire and water' before being re-occupied by those who had been spared its ravages. Like the Biblical lepers, these unclean victims were set apart on the Shore at Leith or the islands of the Forth, and their household effects, it being forbidden by law to wash them in standing water, were placed in the Leith River which it was hoped would carry their impurities like sewage out to sea.

In the last years of the seventeenth century an earlier James Balfour was caught up, along with many others fired with enthusiasm for that ill-omened venture, in the attempt to establish a trading colony in Panama known as the Darien Expedition. To this narrow isthmus of land lying between the Atlantic and Pacific Oceans, apparently so well situated for convenient commerce with the east and west, about four thousand Scotsmen set out in 1698 in search of an elusive fortune. Three ships left Leith on 26th July carrying the colonists. Disease, misfortune and the rivalry of English merchants doomed the enterprise from the beginning, and the sadder and wiser survivors who returned numbered not more than thirty. Several thousands who did not risk their lives but hazarded too much of their worldly wealth reaped a dire financial ruin from which most did not recover. James Balfour, a burgess and guild brother with his business in Leith, had lived in Milne's Court in the Lawnmarket and had had an interest in several commercial enterprises, including ownership of a shipbuilding yard in North Leith and partnership in a Leith soap works. He died, says John Russell, of a broken heart after the Darien misadventure, not realising that all, in fact, had not been lost. By the Treaty of Union of 1707 it was agreed that capital which had been invested in the expedition would be repaid with five per cent interest. These repayments were eventually, if gradually, made good, and James's eldest son, another James, was able to take advantage of this financial return to clear his father's debts and save some portion of his business. By 1719 all the Darien capital had been repaid, and by the previous year James Balfour had known that he was now a rich man. In John Russell's words, he bought forthwith the 'estate of Pilrig with its mansion and park, meadows and cornfields and silvery stream of Broughton Burn'. It was the same innovating James Balfour who obtained a monopoly in Scotland of the manufacture of gunpowder and sited his factory a short distance south-west of Pilrig near the Water of Leith. The area subsequently took its name from these activities, and the later manor house of Powderhall was long outlived by the robust old house of Pilrig.

A footnote was added to the history of the Darien disaster in 1979 when the wreck of the Leith ship the *Olive Branch*, previously known as the *Marion*, was discovered lying in thirty feet of water off Caledonia Bay, near Panama, during a two-year world circumnavigation called 'Operation Drake'. The fully loaded merchant vessel sank in 1700, when nearing the end of her voyage out to the Scottish settlement, when the ship's cooper went below, probably to help himself to some brandy, with a lighted candle which, igniting the spirits, set the *Olive Branch* on fire. Spearheads, cannon balls and Scottish coins were found when the wreck was investigated by divers.

James Balfour of Pilrig was one of the first commissioners to be appointed after the passing, in 1771, of the Act which marked the beginning of enlightened civic administration in Leith. The Act provided for the proper cleansing and lighting of the streets in South Leith, Yardheads and St. Anthony's, as well as the supplying of fresh water to these areas.

It was in Pilrig House, still occupied by the same family, that the Rev. Lewis Balfour, maternal grandfather of Robert Louis Balfour Stevenson, was born in 1777, in later years becoming minister of Colinton Church. On its way towards Pilrig and the sea at Leith, turning many a mill wheel as it went, the industrious little Water flowed, as it flows still, past the manse and garden so well remembered and described by

R.L.S. himself. To his youthful imagination it had been, if not a torrent at the door, more excitingly a haunted stream beyond the garden. 'Down at the corner of the lawn,' he wrote, 'next the snuff-mill, there was a practicable passage through the evergreens, and a door in the wall, which let you out on a small patch of sand, left in the corner by the river. Just across, the woods rose like a wall into the sky; and their lowest branches trailed in the black waters.'

At Stevenson's death in 1894 the Balfour connection with the old family house at Pilrig had only forty-seven years to run. The first step towards its termination was taken in 1920 on the amalgamation of Edinburgh and Leith when, under the Extension Act of that year, the Town Council undertook to provide a public park in close proximity to the Port. Two years later, in fulfilment of this commitment, they acquired over twenty acres of the Pilrig estate, the gift of the house on the death of the liferentress, Miss Margaret Balfour-Melville, being part of the agreement. The conditions attached to this transaction are of considerable interest. The Corporation pledged themselves to the preservation of the building either as a museum or a charitable institution or to use it for some other purpose and never at any time to let it in apartments, divide it into tenements or allow it to fall into disrepair. Miss Balfour-Melville died in 1941 and the house and garden were taken over by the Council with some ceremony and public notice. Contemporary photographs show a well-preserved, lived-in mansionhouse with ivy growing across its walls. A sundial, bearing the words 'The path of the just is as a shining light', was placed at the front of the building on the west wall beneath the sloping roof. The dates 1718-1941 were also incorporated to commemorate the long period of ownership by the Balfours of Pilrig, whose tombs are in South Leith Churchyard.

In the years immediately following these changes the old house saw a diversity of occupants and occupations come and go. At different times it was adapted to meet the varying requirements of a Civil Defence centre, a boys' club and a

Fig. 34.   The surviving shell of Pilrig House after the fire of 1971.

firemen's hostel. In 1946 ten homeless families were given emergency accommodation in the twelve-roomed house, and by 1954 the Corporation let it be known that they could find no further use for it. It stood now without a reason for existence in a public playing field, and vandalism soon hastened its deterioration as doors and windows were broken and, as a consequence, bricked up. It was said that furniture had been piled behind the doors to prevent their being opened, but the contents did not remain inside much longer. Until the end of the 1960s the Corporation maintained a caretaker in solitary residence on an upper floor, but no repairs were ever carried out, and rainwater from the leaking roof put an end to its inhabitability.

For freely accessible, untenanted and decaying property the almost inevitable fate is fire, and in 1971, and again in the following year, the inevitable happened. The roof and upper part of the house, where the most interesting architectural features were located, were destroyed completely, and the resultant ruin was then reduced in size and its remaining walls shored up for safety.

From time to time, both before and after its devastation, various suggestions have been made by interested bodies to revitalise the building with a view to its resumption of some useful role in the community, but because of rising costs and other problems, they have been abandoned. To put flesh once more on the charred bones of Pilrig House would appear a daunting and expensive task, but a proposal to carry out external restoration of the old mansion and to create six flats within the shell of the 1638 building has now been accepted. The plan includes the provision of sheltered housing on adjoining ground and the probable sale of approximately 1.8 acres of Pilrig Park for residential development purposes. Such a scheme, if implemented with sensitivity, could provide a happy alternative to the two hard options between which the house has been hovering for many years — picturesque consolidation as a ruin, or demolition. The lairds of Pilrig, however, the terms of their bequest having been so soon forgotten, might conceivably prefer the latter.

CHAPTER 9
Edinburgh Transport Museum

THE Edinburgh Transport Museum at Shrubhill, in Leith Walk, is well worth a visit, particularly as unconfirmed reports in recent years of its possible closure are now reinforced by a general air of neglect within the four walls of the comparatively small area in which a few fascinating examples of Edinburgh's public transport conveyances are still displayed.

On his entering the Museum, the first vehicles to meet the visitor's eye are likely to be a few parked cars, but these unexpected distractions are soon forgotten in the absorbing interest of the exhibits themselves. The earliest and most delightful of these is a horse-drawn car, painted black and yellow, which plied, as its route board still announces, from Albert Street, via Elm Row and Easter Road, to London Road. Tracks had been laid in Edinburgh and in Leith, then a separate burgh, after the passing of the Tramways Act in 1870, and the first horse cars, replacing the older horse buses which had in their turn replaced the earlier stage coaches, were in operation by the end of the following year. The system, when fully developed, was to service eighteen miles of route with ninety trams and one hundred and ten horses, the drivers working sixty-nine hours each week for which they were paid exactly twenty shillings. A minimum of two horses was required for these cars, but four or five were necessary for some routes, and a trace horse was needed on the city's many steep hills. There was competition for the job of 'trace boy'. The enviable task of these small boys was to ride the extra horse downhill again when the long upward climb had been successfully accomplished.

In the horse tram preserved in the Museum the passengers sat on long continuous seats, facing each other, inside, or on the six double ones on the open top, and the driver mounted to his 'box' by means of two well spaced out steps. Were he to return tomorrow, he would find his whip still in place, convenient to his hand. 'Edinburgh and District Tramways Company Ltd.' is attractively lettered along both sides of the car, together with the name 'John E. Pitcairn, General Manager'. Mr Pitcairn's term of office coincided with the changeover from horse-drawn to cable tramcars, and he superintended the forging of that particular link in the chain of successive vehicles and methods which tell the story of the city's transport history. When examples were being sought for restoration and exhibition in the Museum, this splendid old horse tram was discovered and rescued from a perilous plight of deterioration in Tranent, where it was in use as a chicken run.

Among several small-scale reproductions in the building are models of the cable haulage system, of a Shrubhill-built tramcar which was the forerunner of the standard Edinburgh Corporation Transport cars operating through the streets of Edinburgh from 1934 to 1950, and of a cable car, on loan from the Royal Scottish Museum, indicating the ownership of the original to have been the 'Patent Cable Tramway Corporation Limd'. Many of these cable cars were later converted for use with the subsequent electric system. The Museum's own representative of the cable-car era is almost as attractive visually as the old horse tram and, indeed, the later history of transport illustrates the parallel aesthetic decline which tends to accompany technological advance in every field. Still with an open top, the platform at each end is closed at the side opposite the entrance by a wrought-iron scrollwork panel, and this is complemented by a painted design in black on the narrow, rounded sides of the window frames. These pleasing features symbolise a vanished craftsmanship and personal pride in a well-finished product not likely to be revived in the foreseeable future.

Cable trams were running in Edinburgh from 1888 onwards, but by the early years of the twentieth century the underground mechanism, driven by power stations at various locations in the city, was becoming worn, delays and breakdowns were increasingly frequent and frustrating, and there was growing public dissatisfaction in the Capital. This was not, however, the case in Leith, which had wisely changed its horse trams for an overhead electric traction system, with the result that passengers from Edinburgh had to re-embark at Pilrig Street, where the cables terminated, for the rest of their journey. As a consequence this route was the first to be converted when Edinburgh itself 'went electric', and it was opened on 20th June 1922 for passengers travelling between Pilrig and Liberton. A contemporary photograph shows a huge crowd worthy of a Lord Mayor's Show assembled at the old Leith and Edinburgh boundary to witness the historic event, a number of students predictably jumping on the roof of the now enclosed upper portion of the tram for a free ride. The power station for cable cars on the North Side was the one located in Henderson Row.

Like Lothian Road, which had been constructed in a single day over a hundred years previously, Princes Street was relaid with, albeit temporary, tracks for electric tramcars in a single night, and the work also included the setting up of central poles and overhead wiring. By 1927, 345 electric cars were running in Edinburgh, which had of course included Leith since the general boundary extensions in 1920.

For tarring the road surfaces the Corporation had its own steam rollers, and the Museum is fortunate in having, and displaying, a splendidly conserved example repainted in its original colouring of red and black. Of heavy iron construction, these service vehicles lumbered slowly and noisily along the streets on their enormous wheels, smoke issuing from their tall, black frontal chimney-stalks, like mobile furnaces, which is exactly what they were. To be seen at their best, they had to be seen in action. But the retired veteran in the transport collection is impressive enough, with its iron rake and shovel hanging in readiness towards the rear and a cast brass figure of Britannia clutching her trident above a crouching lion providing the only, and somehow wholly appropriate, decoration at the front.

The interesting interior, however, is not so easily examined, although the levers and handles on the firebox, dated 1910, are reasonably visible. The boiler is another matter, and the metal notice which it carries, to the effect that it must be cleaned thoroughly after every hundred hours of working and that oil and grease must on no account be allowed to get inside, could be read without difficulty only by a contortionist. This problem is explained by the necessity of preventing visitors from entering the vehicles, as they have not always been treated in the past with due respect.

Round the Museum's walls hang a series of photographs depicting transport evolution in the City. One of them shows a First World War conductress standing on her platform beneath a huge advertisement for H.P. Sauce. The advertisements in these old photographs range from the familiar Bovril and Colman's Mustard to such old-fashioned and outdated products as black lead and Rising Sun Stove Polish. 'Graveyard of the Electric Tramway System' is the caption under another which portrays cars being scrapped by a contractor, and the gaily decorated tram which was in fact the last one to be seen in Edinburgh is here also, bearing the legend 'The Last Tram Week' and the relevant dates of 1871 and 1956. Tram drivers' wages at various periods are given among the printed information. In 1950 they earned 2/7½d an hour for a forty-four hour week!

Engrossed in what the Museum has to show, the visitor may forget the telltale signs of dereliction, but they are there nevertheless, and when coming unexpectedly on a shelf, once obviously brightly painted, labelled 'Visitors' Book', from which that item is conspicuously missing, one wonders how long ago it disappeared and what the date of the last entry might have been.

If the Museum ever does have to close, it is greatly to be hoped that another, and perhaps more inviting, location may be found within the City for these unique and excellently preserved survivals which form such a nostalgic, picturesque and irreplaceable record of one aspect of its history.

CHAPTER 10

North Leith

NORTH Leith and South Leith began life as completely separate communities and remained so until comparatively recent times. The latter was in the hands and at the disposal of the Lairds of Restalrig, which was then both a larger and a more important place than the embryonic port, and the former belonged to the Abbey of Holyrood. Because of this association and in reference to the name of the Abbey, North Leith — the area benorth the brig — was known as the 'Rude Side'. One of its enjoinments was to provide fish for the Abbot and canons whose abstention from meat on their frequent fast days was obligatory, and rents, as elsewhere, were then often paid in kind. In the late fifteenth century Abbot Robert Ballantyne built a bridge of 'three stonern arches' over the river, and the street that led from it was the main thoroughfare in North Leith until the provision of a drawbridge at Tolbooth Wynd in 1788 created a new and better one in Bridge Street. As it was a hindrance to shipbuilding, much of which took place on the north side of the Water where the first docks were sited, the old triple-arched crossing was then demolished.

The church of St. Ninian was also built by Abbot Ballantyne at the end of the bridge to spare the inhabitants the long and arduous walk to Holyrood Abbey where they had worshipped until then. St. Ninian's, with its distinctive latticed wooden steeple, later became the parish church of North Leith, and the remains of the building, best seen across the river from The Shore, are still a conspicuous feature in the Leith townscape. It was not replaced as the parish church until 1813.

When the new Georgian North Leith Church, designed by William Burn, was built in Madeira Street in that year, its graceful spire rose from the surrounding fields as it rises now above the well worn streets and buildings of its present environment. A much older foundation, however, was the Hospital, with its chapel and burying ground, of St. Nicholas, the patron saint of seamen, which disappeared in the mid-seventeenth century when Cromwell's Citadel obliterated all else on the ancient site. North Leith had laid its citizens to rest in St. Nicholas' churchyard, and to compensate for its loss the City of Edinburgh gave them 'a garden extending to the river bank' in Coburg Street, to quote John Russell, which served as the only cemetery until the opening of Warriston in 1843 and Rosebank three years later. Robert Nicoll, known as the Keats of Scottish poets as he died in his early twenties, is buried in the Coburg Street ground, and near the gate is an altar-tomb to Thomas Gladstone (grandfather of the Victorian statesman), who was an elder in North Leith Church.

The Citadel was erected on the beach with the salt spray flung against its walls in rough weather, but the sea has gradually been banished further away. This fortification was granted by the restored king to the Earl of Lauderdale who called the complex of buildings, in the Monarch's honour, Charlestown. But the Earl soon disposed of it to — predictably — the City of Edinburgh, and the houses it contained were then let out. Various commercial ventures were set up within its confines, including a glassworks, and it had a history of many different uses and adaptations until its final demolition. The arched pend of the principal entrance on the east side is all that survives to the present day.

After the Reformation in 1560 the ecclesiastical overlordship in North Leith was superseded (together with St. Leonards, on the south side of the river, and most of the village of Broughton) by the secular superiority of the Earl of Roxburgh. Canongate was also in the Earl's possession, and he sold it, along with North Leith, to the Governors of George Heriot's Hospital, from whom the latter passed in 1639 to the Town Council and Magistrates of the City of Edinburgh.

In 1780 a ship known as the *Fury* was constructed at North Leith, and it was at that spot, in 1812, in what is now Commercial Street, that the Customs House was built, in the prevailing Grecian style, to the designs of Robert Reid, one of the architects of the Second New Town of Edinburgh and the last of the King's Architects in Scotland. It had previously been situated, in very inferior premises, in Tolbooth Wynd.

CHAPTER 11
Landward Leith

BEFORE the North Bridge was built in the second half of the eighteenth century, the journey to Leith from Old Edinburgh on its ridge of rock was a daunting and hazardous undertaking. The precipitous northern slope of the ridge, at the foot of which lay the valley between it and the Calton Hill which corresponded with the Cowgate valley on the other or southern side, had first to be negotiated and, to facilitate an easier access to the Port, the steep, descending street known as Leith Wynd was consequently constructed. It was in fact a continuation, across the High Street, of St. Mary's Wynd which climbed the hill from the south, the Netherbow Port, which marked the boundary between the city and the separate burgh of Canongate, standing at the junction of the two thoroughfares. The cross streets followed the line of an ancient Roman road.

At the bottom of Leith Wynd, on opposite sides of the street, stood the Trinity College Church and Hospital founded in 1462 by Mary of Gueldres, Queen of James II, and the old charitable workhouse known as Paul's Work erected by the city magistrates in 1479 when, according to contemporary records, sterner methods were used to persuade 'ydill people to betake themselves to sum Vertew and Industrie' than are deemed appropriate now. Paul's Work, founded by Bishop Spence of Aberdeen and dedicated to the Virgin, was afterwards used for the unlikely twin purposes of a woollen manufactory and a house of correction. This old and picturesque group of buildings was sacrificed to the North British Railway in the nineteenth century, although the apse of the Trinity Church was re-erected near the Old Town on higher and safer ground below the ridge. Through the gate, or port, which closed the Wynd at this point, the burgh of Calton was entered at its principal street, St. Ninian's or, significantly, Beggars' Row, where for long had stood beside the way the chapel dedicated to St. Ninian. A narrow lane or close known as the Salt Backet ran off St. Ninian's Row and in it another chapel, a small Methodist meeting-house standing, says Grant, 'almost in the direct line of the Regent Arch' in Waterloo Place on the hillside above, was built by the Wesleyans. The Row skirted the Hill and its outcrops which were then devoid of monuments and are shown on some early maps as McNeill's Craigs.

The Barony of Calton or Caldtoun was owned in the seventeenth century by Lord Balmerino, of the Elphinstone family, who in the same century purchased the building, afterwards known as Balmerino House, in which Charles II had found lodging in the Kirkgate of Leith during his 'Scottish adventure' of 1650 when he had little choice but to support the Presbyterian cause in order to restore the monarchy. The Church of Our Lady Star of the Sea was built in the grounds of Balmerino House in 1853. As time has told, it was with Leith that the history of the Burgh of Calton — a name which had many variants including Craigend, Craigingalt and Galttoun — was to be most closely linked. A charter of 1725 reveals that the lands of Calton, Back of Canongate and Yardheads of Leith, having been part of the Barony of Restalrig, were at that date made over to the Burgh of Edinburgh. The origin of the name Craigend is of some interest. In the Middle Ages the parish of South Leith encompassed a loch, the water of which was later used to provide the houses of Leith with their first supply of piped water, and a craig or hill. The loch end of the parish became known as Lochend, and Craigend was the name given to the other end of the parish at the Calton Hill.

About forty years ago a short history of 'the Calton' was written by a well-known 'indweller', as he called himself, Mr Francis Caird Inglis, who succeeded his father in the long line of pioneer photographers at Rock House on the Calton Hill which had started in the 1840s with David Octavius Hill, whose early calotypes are so much prized today. Quoting from the Parish Registers of South Leith, he tells how, in 1643, a bailie and elders from 'Lastelrig [Restalrig] and Caldtoune' were ordained to 'take up a list of ye fencible persones' in both localities, a reference to the efforts then being made by the Scottish Church to enlist in the Covenanting Army all those who were capable of bearing firearms. The Covenant was sworn 'by both man and woman' as a congregation in December 1648, and on Christmas Eve intimation was made that they should come to 'subscrive ye same' the following Tuesday 'after sermon'. Before the advent of newspapers it was common practice for items of local and national interest to be intimated from parish pulpits, the latter often to inform the people of Acts which had been passed by Parliament.

Almost twenty years later the members of South Leith Church were reminded of their 'Saboth day' instructions in a report from the Presbytery read out by the minister. 'No boats barks or any uyr vessells' should 'sail out the harbour upon the Lord's day under paine of censur both civil and ecclesiastick', no persons should be found drawing water from the wells and carrying it to their houses, and no-one must 'vaige' upon the shore 'efter ye afternoon's sermon' or in any street in Restalrig or Craigend 'under paine of lyk censur'.

By 1674 the steeple was in need of 're-edifying', and the concurrence in an appeal for contributions towards its repair was sought from the Session and the Laird of Craigentinnie, who at that time was either Sir Patrick Nisbet, who had been created a baronet of Nova Scotia in 1669 (the ground now covered by the Castle Esplanade having been 'converted' into the soil of that country for the purpose of selling baronetcies), or his second cousin, Alexander, with whom he exchanged the estate of Craigentinnie for that of Dean. In 1682, to settle a quarrel, Alexander Nisbet left the country, and on his return was promptly imprisoned in the Tolbooth, together with his opponent, for taking part in a duel.

In 1695 permission was given, surprisingly, for the

inhabitants of Calton to 'bury ye dead' upon 'ye Sabath'. They might do so, 'if they please', between sermons, provided that in winter they were at the churchyard 'before two hours chap in ye clock of South Leith'.

There is an amusing entry in the records of July 1696. It had become a practice in the reformed church in Scotland, when they were not in use, to lock the box-seats of those members who were of substance in the community, and an official pew-opener with sets of keys was always in attendance before services. The key-keeper 'of ye Caltoun seats' appears to have abused his office by refusing to open the pews of certain gentlemen until after 'Sermon was begun' because they 'would not give him money'. For this offence he was appointed 'to be summoned to ye Session'.

The Barony of Calton had its own Baron Bailie and its honorary constables from whom subsequently developed the Society of High Constables of Calton in the early nineteenth century. It had also the right to hold its own Beltane Day celebrations which took place each year in early May and over which the Baron Bailie presided attired in his robes and badge of office. For the enforcement of law and order in the district the Calton drummer, when occasion demanded it, went sounding through the streets with civic proclamations, one such occasion in 1772 being for the purpose of dissuading the local apprentices from throwing stones and mobbing, and another four years later being in order 'to prevent persons from bickering on the Calton hill'. His remuneration for carrying out this duty was two shillings. Public services of this nature were probably in frequent demand, as repairs to 'the Calton drum' became necessary around this time. In 1816 the burgh acquired an association with the 'immortal memory' when Burns' Clarinda, Mrs Maclehose, went to live on the upper floor of a tenement house in the little street called Calton Hill.

This was an area rich in natural springs, and its indwellers were consequently much more easily supplied with water than the inhabitants of the Old Town itself, who were hard put to it to keep the dirty closes and the high, over-populated 'lands' in any state approaching cleanliness.

'Until Waterloo Place and Regent's Bridge' — the former to commemorate the victorious battle of 1815 and the latter to compliment the Prince Regent who later entered Edinburgh by this route as George IV — 'were opened', wrote John Geddie, 'the Calton Hill was reached by descending into the depths of Low Calton and climbing up the steep and narrow path of Craigend.' The new roadway to the east and south was driven through the Calton burial ground as relentlessly as a few years later the railway ironware of the Age of Steam was to be thrust through the quiet hollow in which were situated Paul's Work and the Trinity College Church, the remnants of St. Ninian's Chapel being destroyed when the ground was cleared for the building of the Regent's Arch. Leith Wynd itself, overtaken by the tide of nineteenth-century redevelopment and 'improvement', became the site, to quote the same historian of Edinburgh, of 'railway platforms, sidings and signal boxes'. Geology being more impervious to change than the works of man, only the rocks and the everlasting hills remain.

CHAPTER 12

Perils of the Port

IN the year 1622, in the first week of June, there were alarms and excursions in the port of Leith. Three foreign ships 'in the heart of Leith harbour', as James Grant describes the incident, were varying by a sea-fight the usual 'excitements of the times'. At this period the mutual enmity between Spain and Holland was so strong that the presence together in a neutral port of Dutch and Spanish ships could lead to a dangerous confrontation which the port authorities were hard put to it to control.

The Spanish frigate was about peaceful purposes enough. Being in no hurry to take on board their required provisions, the crew went ashore as they felt inclined. But when two 'vessels of War', commanded by the Admiral of Zealand, anchored alongside them, the situation changed quickly and dramatically for the worse during a night which would not soon be forgotten in the Port. At dawn the battle of the boats was causing such 'terror and confusion' among the inhabitants that the burgesses 'rushed to arms and armour' and, although the Water Bailie accompanied by a herald commanded 'both parties to forbear hostilities in Scottish waters', attack and counter-attack 'continued with unabated fury until midnight'.

The Spanish captain, having at his disposal the artillery of one ship only, got the worst of it as the 'Dutchmen poured their broadsides upon his shattered hull', and even that tough old race of seadogs the mariners of Leith were, as one authority reported, 'altogether unable . . . to enforce obedience'. The burgesses were now obliged to bring 'ordonance from the Castell to the shoare to ding at them'. Cannoniers with a battery of guns came down with all speed 'by the Bonnington Road most probably' but arrived too late to save the Spaniards who had been bombarded out of the harbour where their vessel ran aground 'after great slaughter' on the Black Rocks, 'then known as the Mussel Cape'. A party of Leith seamen went on board and raised the Scottish flag, hoping that the Dutch would have at least some respect for the emblem of Scottish sovereignty, but it had no effect: the truculent Dutchmen 'boarded her in the night, burned her to the water's edge, and sailed away before dawn'.

Fortunately incidents of such immediate danger were the exception rather than the rule, but Leith has experienced her full share of storm and skaith throughout the stirring years of history.

The Siege of Leith during the Wars of the Reformation, when the Lords of the Congregation, assisted by the Protestant English, turned their force of arms against the Catholic Queen Regent, supported by the French, in the beleaguered Port, threw up perils in plenty for the luckless population. In the mid-seventeenth century, when Cromwell, after the Battle of Dunbar, succeeded in taking control of Edinburgh and Leith, he delegated to General Monk the task of strengthening the Port's defences. So Monk built the Citadel 'benorth the brig' from the bastions of which, however, few guns were ever fired in anger. The later Napoleonic Wars at the end of the eighteenth century threatened much greater havoc with the prospect of a French invasion. To defend the harbour entrance a stone Martello tower (now on reclaimed land in the Docks area) was constructed at a cost of £17,000 on the same Mussel Cape rock that had seen the final undoing of the old Spanish frigate. The name of these towers, erected along the east coast at this period, was a corruption of Mortella Point in Corsica where a similar defensive structure had withstood a British cannonade in 1794.

The sea itself was a continuing hazard, especially in fogs and storms, and it was not until well into the nineteenth century that efficient and reliable lights were placed in the Forth for the guidance of shipping, which had to pay a levy known as 'light money' to defray their cost. In the late 1700s

Fig. 35.   The Martello Tower at Leith, built at sea and now on reclaimed land at the Docks.

coal lights burned on the May and other islands, but were often mistaken for fires at limekilns and pits on land, and oil lights with rotating and reflecting glasses were not in use until the early years of the following century. The merchants of the Port contributed £150 towards the cost of erecting a beacon on the Bell Rock in 1803, but it was swept away by gales in the ensuing winter. Lighthouses were expensive and dangerous to build, and progress was held back by lack of funds.

As in all large ports, there was a constant risk of importing infectious diseases from foreign crews and insanitary vessels until late in the nineteenth century, and Leith was fortunate in escaping lightly from the ever-present danger of epidemic outbreaks. An alarming and unexpected warning of these possibilities occurred as late as 1905 when a labourer employed by the Corporation, his wife and their two children were found to be suffering from plague. The woman worked for a rag dealer in squalid premises but the source of the illness was never definitely traced. Though the rest of his family recovered, and no-one else appears to have been affected, the labourer died in Pilton Isolation Hospital, more familiar today as the Northern General. The last and most virulent visitation of Bubonic plague to Edinburgh and Leith in epidemic proportions was in 1645 when 2736 people died in the Port, more than half the population. John Russell writes of the 'terror and distress in Leith', with 'death and desolation in every street', as the previous harvest had failed, and the dreaded 'pest', as it was called, usually followed famine. An attempt was made to cleanse the filth from the streets. Dead swine and the contents of middens were taken in carts to the sands and placed within reach of the tide. On the Links 'great trenches' were dug to receive mass burials, and the remains of these plague victims have been discovered from time to time ever since when the foundations of new buildings have been laid, especially near Wellington Place where the greatest number were interred. For a whole year the people suffered the ravages of this dire disease which had started in April. It abated somewhat in the cold of the succeeding winter but reappeared spasmodically until, with the coming again of Spring in the following year, it finally died away at the end of the most desperate twelve months in the history of Leith. A pair of inscribed silver cups was presented to South Leith Church by the two bailies 'in tyme of pest', and these thank offerings are still in regular use.

Cholera and typhoid fever were both periodic causes of concern. The ravages of cholera on an epidemic scale in Edinburgh and Leith were last experienced in 1866, and typhoid or enteric fever gradually decreased as science and the twentieth century advanced.

In October 1866 the efforts of authority to contain the menacing cholera outbreak met with an astonishingly fatalistic response from the community. The neighbours of those who had died from the disease would not be deterred from crowding into their houses, presumably to condole with remaining relatives, and when remonstrated with by an official, one of them is said to have replied, 'Do you think you can stop the hands of the Almighty? If our time has come you cannot prevent us from being seized'. The first Medical Officer of Health in Edinburgh, Dr, later Sir, Henry Duncan Littlejohn, had been apointed in 1862, and the *Leith Burghs Pilot*, which responsibly reported the course of the epidemic, noted that, in the doctor's opinion, this attitude showed 'not only an amount of ignorance but a degree of recklessness that all must deplore'. It put on record the new Health official's urgent plea for volunteers to undertake a house-to-house visitation in Leith, one of the areas where the outbreak was most severe, in order to 'lead the people to have better ideas on this subject'.

Contraction of the disease was largely confined to the poorer parts of the city, and as clothing purchased from pawnbrokers was considered particularly liable to spread infection, the 'more respectable' pawnbrokers in the Port were interviewed 'to see what could be done in that respect'. Curiously, another dangerous practice was thought to be 'the use of hard ale', and 'its sale had been given up by every respectable establishment in Leith'. One vendor who had been in the Port for thirteen years told how he 'had seen his customers rapidly dying since cholera came to Leith', all 'apparently strong and healthy men'.

Even the vagrants were a menace to the law-abiding working inhabitants to whom they importunately appealed for charity. In South Leith in early times the genuine beggars were given numbered badges to distinguish them from their fraudulent counterparts and were thus licensed to beg unhindered so long as they did not 'cross the bridge' to the Rude Side, at which point the writ of South Leith Church

Kirk Session, who authorised and provided the badges, ceased to run. They also appointed a staffman 'to hold the sturdy beggars out of ye towne' but were never entirely successful in ridding the parish of these idle vagabonds who went about in gangs and knew only too well how to 'exercise the wits of the authorities' while continuing to live satisfactorily on their own.

As late as the opening years of the twentieth century the lot of the poor was still a hard and often a hopeless one. In 1909 the *Leith Observer* announced an enquiry into the system of punishment at the Poorhouse, declaring it to be 'a scandal on the part of any efficient Parish Council to send a man to break stones in a close cell at Seafield'. Such places were now to be properly ventilated following a recent incident in which a cell door had been broken down for air by its incarcerated inmate, for which offence he had humanely been let off. It was apparently considered 'that breaking stones was not a punishment but a recognised system of testing cases', and as the man had had over thirty Police Court convictions, he was therefore a test case. Eight recipients of Poorhouse 'charity' had in one afternoon preferred to leave rather than endure conditions created within the cells by ventilation of the kind provided by a quarter-inch space between the closed door and the ground!

The perils of life in the Port were not all of the dire and solemn variety — though small offences were liable to be countered by swift punishments much too stern to fit the crime or the criminals who were often motivated by deprivation and genuine need. On one occasion, prompted by either need or greed, a thief stole the watch-coat in a watch-house from a sleeping watchman, and those invested with the power to mete out justice left the culprit in no doubt about his fate if he were apprehended. He was to be summarily hanged in the watch-house and consigned to the graveyard at South Leith Church. There is no record of the sentence being carried out, but there is of a watchdog being placed in the watch-house to watch the watchmen and their watch-coats, and of an undertaking to keep a most extraordinary and vigilant watch in future inside the watch-house!

The supernatural was sometimes blamed for nocturnal terrors, even when aided and abetted by the demon drink, and there were those who would rather spend a night in the churchyard than walk down St. Anthony's Lane of a dark winter evening. It was here that Green Jenny used to haunt the passers-by till their blood ran cold, and they could never forget the night when the shoemaker, as he himself had recounted it, had left a tavern in the Kirkgate and come face to face in St. Anthony's Lane with a mortcloth standing on end. This was a singular spectacle no doubt, but he had no intention of being frightened of 'twa-three yairds o' green velvet'. The next moment he was completely enveloped by it and, as it smelled undeniably of the charnel-house, shook it off as best he could with trembling hands. Suddenly, standing in front of him, he found a beautiful angel, but the worthy citizen had had enough and took to his heels, which soon carried him out of St. Anthony's Lane.

But Jenny was flesh and blood no less than the shoemaker. Her husband was a brewer in a small way of business who had had the misfortune to become bankrupt but had also had the blessing of a shrewd and hard-working wife. She laboured early and late at the brewery in St. Anthony's Lane, preserving it, when he was 'roupit', from the creditors who were eventually repaid in full. Dressed in a long, white apron over which she threw a large velvet cloak of many folds, she kept a watchful eye on the business premises at night. After her death there were no more ghosts in the Lane, and the solid denizens of Leith could return unhaunted, if still unsteadily, to their homes.

During the Second World War Leith Docks were singled out as a potential target by the German Air Force. In 1940 and 1941 there were several deaths and injuries in the Port as a result of bombs falling in George Street, Portland Place and a site near Leith Hospital, which was fortunately undamaged, as were the Docks themselves.

The last decade or two have witnessed the appearance of an alarming amount of dereliction in Leith due to the wiping out of buildings, many of them dwellinghouses, on a scale far greater than might have been expected from an air raid. The enemy this time was within, when lack of foresight combined with lack of funds to bring about the planning blight which has so harmfully affected Leith and the South Side of Edinburgh. The rebuilding of the Port will doubtless produce, if not its perils, at least its pressures and its problems, and it is earnestly to be hoped that Leith does not lose its historic personality in the process.

CHAPTER 13

Poets of the Port

LIKE Oxford with her dreaming spires, Edinburgh City, New and Old, the Modern Athens, the Northern Temple of the Winds, has never suffered the neglect of poets. It was Scott's 'own romantic town', Tennyson's 'grey metropolis of the north' and the 'fair city' of Allan Ramsay. But Leith of the sea and the ships that do business in the great waters, as the ancient carved stone declares from the walls of Trinity House, in the Kirkgate, has not by any means been bypassed by the Muse.

Robert Fergusson, whose genius flowered briefly and ended tragically in the City, is now well-known for his poems on the Port. His comic celebration of 'Leith Races', using various local dialects of the old Scots language, vividly describes an obviously familiar and highly relished experience in suitably robust rhyme. The first verses set the scene and then he goes on to capture in a colourful word-picture the public holiday atmosphere among the crowd making its noisy, high-spirited way to Leith:

> Quo' she, I ferly unco sair,
> That ye sud musin gae;
> Ye who hae sung o' Hallow-fair,
> Her Winter's pranks, and play;
> Whan on Leith sands the racers rare
> Wi' Jocky louns are met,
> Their orra pennies there to ware,
> And drown themselves in debt,
>   Fu' deep that day.

> . . .

> We'll reel and ramble thro' the sands,
> And jeer wi' a' we meet;
> Nor hip the daft and gleesome bands
> That fill Edina's street
>   Sae thrang this day.

117

. . .

> Ere servant-maids had wont to rise
> To seethe the breakfast kettle,
> Ilk dame her brawest ribbons tries,
> To put her on her mettle.

. . .

> Here is the true and faithfu' list
> O' Noblemen and Horses;
> Their eild, their weight, their height, their grist,
> That rin for plates or purses
>   Fu' fleet this day.

The Town Guard, their uniforms and themselves well washed and brushed for the occasion, are much in evidence and proud of their responsibility for the safe arrival of the purse for which there will later be fierce and exuberant competition:

> To town guard drum of clangour clear,
> Baith men and steeds are raingit;
> Some liveries red or yellow wear,
> And some are tartan spraingit.

The games and excitements, the shrill voices of the ale-wives and the Aberdeen fish sellers and the whole boisterous spectacle are all recorded as if they had taken place the day before, and then, the long-anticipated hours of freedom and amusement over for another year, the homeward exodus from Leith gets under way:

> The races ower, they hale the dools
> Wi' drink o' a kinkind;
> Great feck gae hirplin hame, like fools,
> The cripple lead the blind.

The races continued to be held for almost a hundred years after Fergusson's time, but by 1862 they were over for good. The racecourse on the sands then became the site of the Albert Dock, which was opened in 1869, thirteen years after the Victoria Dock, obliterating 84 acres of the sea shore.

Fergusson is best known for his vernacular poetry and his

eulogies on ardent spirits, but he wrote in English as well in the approved eighteenth-century style and even devoted an entire poem to the praise of tea. But his lively pen and livelier mind were active for only a few brief years; he died, aged 24, in the miserable and squalid old Bedlam, near the Bristo Port in Edinburgh, and it was reaction to the wretched circumstances of his death that led Professor Andrew Duncan to open a new, humanitarian institution for the mentally ill at Morningside, when the old prison-like, forbidding Bedlam was done away with. Fergusson was buried in the Canongate Churchyard, and it was Robert Burns, in acknowledgement of his debt to the earlier bard, who had a stone placed above the unmarked grave at his own expense.

As a local poet Edinburgh has claimed Fergusson as her own, but it is perhaps not widely remembered now that Leith has her own particular poet as well in the person of Robert Gilfillan, copies of whose work (inferior, it must be said, to that of Fergusson) are rarely come across today. He was not a native of the Port, having been born in 1798 in Dunfermline, but he became resident there later and was appointed Collector of Police Rates in Leith. He died in 1850, and a monumental stone to his memory, says John Russell, was placed in South Leith Churchyard.

In 1831 his *Original Songs*, dedicated to Allan Cunningham — a fellow-poet and the 'honest Allan' of Sir Walter Scott — were published by, among others, James Burnet of Leith. In the introduction to his collected works he claimed to 'enter the lists as no competitor to Burns, Tannahill or MacNeill, but merely as a humble follower — not as a belted earl but as a 'lowly squire''. Had a better education been available to him, he thought, 'the work would probably have presented fewer inelegancies of language'. On the subject of Leith itself, he wrote a parody called 'The Half-Drowned Tar':

> Along by the banks of Leith's ancient harbour
> Jack Oakum reeled drunk from a dive on the shore,
> O' whither, they cried, dost thou steer so to larboard?
> When plump, from the quay-side he quickly fell o'er!

E

After managing to grab a rope, Jack was pulled from the water. Though his purse was no longer 'with sovereigns full swimming' that he'd 'earned in the war', his rescuers 'hied him away to a tavern' but could not persuade the landlord to draw him rum without payment. Jack had sufficient strength left to floor both them and the landlord, all of whom promptly 'ran like the devil from the half-drowned tar'.

Gilfillan seems to have had a particular bent for writing parody, and the famous 'Blue Bonnets' inspired his verses in praise of Sir Walter Scott:

> Read, read, Woodstock and Waverley,
> Turn every page and read forward in order;
> Read, read, every tale cleverly,
> All the old novels are over the border!

It was the great Battle of 1815, however (at which time he was only 17 years old and may perhaps have written the lines at a later date) that drew from the Poet of Leith, who was favourably mentioned in the renowned *Noctes Ambrosianae* — a fact which must have given him considerable satisfaction — his most stirring verses:

> The trump of war hath ceased to blow,
> And Britain hath no more a foe;
> The sword is sheathed that Scotia drew,
> That gleamed so red on Waterloo.
> That morn, unclouded, rose the sun,
> Our army, too, in brightness shone;
> But night displayed another view,
> When all was still on Waterloo.
>
> . . .
>
> The trumpet sounds, but ne'er again
> Shall Scotia's warriors hear the strain;
> They sleep, but not on their mountains blue,
> The heroes' bed is Waterloo!
> Britannia weeps for many a son,
> And a wail is heard in Caledon
> For the gallant youths, so brave and true,
> Who, fighting, fell on Waterloo!

CHAPTER 14

Famous Sons of Leith

AN Edinburgh historian whose name is not as well kown now as it used to be is Hugo Arnot, a conspicuous eccentric character in the city in the eighteenth century. His father was a shipmaster in Leith called Pollock, and Robert Chambers, in his *Traditions of Edinburgh*, states that he took the name of Arnot from a small inheritance in Fife. His son was acclaimed as a chronicler in 1779 when his *History of Edinburgh* was published, a work which was written when he was under 30 years of age. In 1772 he had entered at the bar and, in the Edinburgh of the 1780s, was the only advocate then residing in the New Town. His house was in Meuse Lane, off St. Andrew Street, where he lived with a manservant during the last few years of his foreshortened life. He was a victim of asthma and a chronic cough which he suspected would one day carry him off like a rocket, which in fact it did, at the age of 37, in 1786.

Poor Hugo's illness was responsible for his having an extremely irritable disposition which tended to exasperate some of his associates, and it was on account of this that he found it necessary to place the prospectuses, or preliminary notices, for another literary work, his *Criminal Trials*, in the coffee houses to bring them to the attention of the public, as the booksellers would have nothing to do with them. His skeletal appearance was the subject of much legal leg-pulling, and John Geddie has preserved one example which was often quoted at the time. The East Pier at Leith had become a favourite promenade, and 'all that was learned and brilliant in the Edinburgh and Leith society of former days have paced here — Burns and Scott and Carlyle among them', and Hugo Arnot riving at his speldrin and looking, as the Parliament House wit said, "Like his meat"'. This cryptic remark was intended to convey an observed similarity between the skin and bone of Hugo's asthmatic person and a dried haddock he had been gnawing in the street — a practice not usually associated by future generations with judicial dignity! This learned legal scarecrow combined two notable characteristics of his profession during the eighteenth century — a leaning towards letters and a highly outlandish and individual personality.

Mention the name of Gladstone and every schoolboy will, or until fairly recently certainly would, associate it with one of the great Prime Ministers of Queen Victoria's reign. Although he was brought up and educated in England, he must surely rank, if not as a famous son, at least as a famous grandson of the Port. The family history began in Clydesdale where, according to James Grant, they claimed descent from an 'ancient and not undistinguished stock'. Mr John Gladstones of Toftcombes, near Biggar, in the upper ward of Clydesdale, had by his wife Janet Aitken a son called Thomas who became a prosperous trader in Leith as a flour and barley merchant in the Coal Hill, married Helen, daughter of Mr Walter Neilson of Springfield, and died in 1809. Of that marriage John Gladstone, father of the future statesman, was the eldest son.

John, later Sir John, was born in 1764 in 'the rather gloomy Coal Hill of Leith', and grew up in the area around it and Sheriff Brae. After moving to Liverpool, he acquired a considerable fortune, his Leith apprenticeship standing him in good trading stead, and also became known, through generous gifts of money to the Church of England, as a philanthropist and benefactor. Success having crowned his career in the south, the lure of his native country brought him back to Scotland where he continued his liberality to the Scottish Episcopal Church. He took an active interest in the political controversies of his time, wielding his pen against the repeal of the Corn Laws, and 'desire was more than once expressed to see him in Parliament'. After several unsuccessful attempts, he was elected Conservative Member for Lancaster in 1819. During the years 1821 to 1826 he represented

Woodstock, and finally, in 1827, the town of Berwick. On the recommendation of Sir Robert Peel, he was created a baronet in 1846.

Sir John had several children by his second wife, Anne Robertson, daughter of Andrew Robertson, Provost of Dingwall. They called their youngest son William Ewart. Born in 1809, he was destined for greater and more enduring parliamentary fame than that to which his father could lay claim. His father had, nevertheless, risen to the status of a country gentleman with the acquisition of a 'beautiful seat' at Fasque, in the Howe of the Mearns, and it was here that he died on 7th December 1851 aged 86.

William Ewart Gladstone held many offices in Government and was four times Chancellor of the Exchequer. Leaving the Conservative Party to join the Liberals, he became Liberal leader in 1867 and Prime Minister a year later. He retired in 1874 but disagreed so violently with the subsequent Consevative administration's policies that he embarked on his famous Midlothian campaign and set a precedent for politicians of the future by declaiming his election oratory from the rear platform of a Pullman train as he travelled north. As a result of his efforts he was back in office by 1880. The last four years of his life were spent in retirement and the study of theology before his death in 1898. James Grant reminds us that 'Gladstone Place, near the Links, has been so named in honour of this family'.

Another, if perhaps less well remembered, native of the Port was John Home, author of the early Scottish historical play called *Douglas*. In September 1724 he was born in the burgh's Quality Street in a house on the east side and near the northern end, as Grant, always including as much detailed information as he could find, has recorded. His father, Alexander Home, was Town Clerk of Leith and had married Christian, the daughter of an Edinburgh family called Hay. Their son John attended the Kirkgate Grammar School and completed his education at the University of Edinburgh where he studied for the ministry. On his father's side he was

descended from Sir James Home of Cowdenknowes who was
an ancestor of the Earls of Home. In the present century this
family has produced a modern playwright, William Douglas
Home, as well as Sir Alec Douglas Home, a recent Prime
Minister.

After being licensed by the Edinburgh Presbytery in 1745,
John Home temporarily abandoned his chosen profession and
joined the corps of volunteers being assembled to confront
that most famous Prince of Scottish history who was, in that
equally famous year, about to advance on the ancient capital
of his forefathers. Charles was on his southern, successful,
march and, sweeping on with sanguine prospects, dreamt not
yet of his defeat. It was the luckless volunteers who were
undone at Falkirk, where Home was captured and cast into
custody by the Stuart Army at Doune Castle. But its stone
walls did not 'for long a prison make' for the young and
energetic John who, along with several other Hanoverian
soldiers who had been taken with him, made good their
escape by the time-honoured method of tying blankets into
ropes and climbing down out of a window. Carrying with
them a comrade injured in the descent from their stronghold,
they set out for Alloa, where a sloop called the *Vulture* was
about to sail for South Queensferry. From there it was a
short, safe journey back to Leith and home.

The following year, resuming his clerical vocation, he was
called as minister to a church in Athelstaneford where he
carried out his pastoral duties for about ten years, and it was
during this period that he discovered his talent as a
playwright, possibly prompted by the unusual circumstance
that his predecessor in the charge, Robert Blair, had been an
author. *Agis*, the first of Home's tragedies, was offered in
1749 to the actor David Garrick, who made it clear he was
not impressed with it and turned it down, and it was not until
1755 that *Douglas*, based on an old ballad called 'Gil Morice',
was completed. This time he decided to go to London himself
and, with the play in his pocket, the divine-turned-dramatist
rode south on horseback personally to present his play to

Garrick. But Garrick did not think much of *Douglas* either and told the disappointed author he considered it was 'totally unfit for the stage'.

The Rev. John Home now turned his hopes and his attention to a theatrical personality in his native Scotland called West Digges, and the play which was to cause such a storm of controversy and to bring enormous fame to its creator was produced in Edinburgh by Digges in a theatre at the bottom of a close in the Canongate on 14th December 1756, as Robert Chambers noted in his *Traditions*. About two years later it was put on at Covent Garden with Peg Woffington, three years before her death, in the principal female part, and the play continued in unabated popularity for over half a century. In 1950 *Douglas* was performed at the Edinburgh Festival with Dame Sybil Thorndike, over 150 years after the previous production.

Denounced by a Church which saw acting and playwriting by one of its ministers as outrageous, Home decided to resign his charge in East Lothian and devote himself to composing tragedies for the theatre of his day. Deprived of his livelihood, no doubt he was grateful for the annual pension of £300 awarded him by George III, although he was not without some 'sinecure appointments', as Grant calls them, and he was certainly well enough off to be able to support a wife, 'a lady of his own name', whom he married after settling in Edinburgh in 1779. Their 'neat little house' was in North Hanover Street and the actress Mrs Sarah Siddons, when appearing in the City, 'spent an occasional afternoon with Mr and Mrs Home' with whom she usually had an early dinner served by Home's old manservant John.

The playwright counted David Hume, Adam Smith and Dr Alexander Carlyle among his literary friends, and he was one of the subjects of Kay's celebrated caricatures or *Portraits*. He was a captain in the Duke of Buccleuch's Fencibles and never fully recovered from falling from his horse, an accident which took place when he was on parade. This prominent old character of eighteenth-century Edinburgh reached his 84th year notwithstanding, and the seaport claimed him as her own again when he died and was buried in the churchyard of South Leith Church on the western side. A commemorative tablet beside his grave is inscribed 'In memory of John Home, author of the tragedy of "Douglas" etc. Born 13th September 1724. Died 4th September 1808'.

James Grant, however, calls this early example of Scottish dramatic writing 'a rather dull work' which had nevertheless 'maintained a certain popularity', and praises instead a history of the Jacobite Rebellion, 'the task of his declining years', which was published in London in 1802. But it is by *Douglas* that Home has been remembered by all subsequent generations and, as Henry Mackenzie (who preserved many biographical details of his fellow-writer in his Memoirs) is always associated with one book, *The Man of Feeling*, so are John Home and *Douglas* names that are likely to remain inseparable in Scotland's literary annals.

Though by no means a native of Leith, Hugh Miller had several encounters with the Port, but they are of sufficient interest to be given a chapter to themselves.

CHAPTER 15

Hugh Miller and Leith

HUGH Miller, the Cromarty stonemason, eminent geologist, newspaper editor and writer, was born in 1802 in the thatched and whitewashed cottage in Cromarty that has since become a place of pilgrimage and, more recently, a tourist attraction in the North-East of Scotland. This sailor's son who laid bare the mysteries of the Old Red Sandstone in his book, probably his best known work, of that name spent a large part of his life in Edinburgh and related the experiences he had during earlier visits there in his biographical masterpiece, *My Schools and Schoolmasters*.

It was in fact an unusual inheritance that first brought the young Hugh Miller to the south — unusual in that it was an inheritance of which he and his family wanted to rid themselves rather than to possess. The bequest had been to his father and consisted of a ground-floor flat in 'an old brick building four storeys in height', as he later described it, in the Coal Hill in Leith, but as he had died when Hugh was only five years old, nothing could be done about disposing of this vexatious property until Hugh himself, as the son of the beneficiary, had come of age. To begin with, it had provided a small income in rent as it was let as a public house and tap-room, but alterations to the harbour, which resulted in the shipping lying at Coal Hill being brought instead to a lower stretch of the Water of Leith, put an abrupt stop to the business and the rent was reduced by half, the remainder being frequently left unpaid by various 'miserable tenants'.

Mr Veitch, the Town Clerk of Leith and the family's house agent there, wrote 'brief curt letters' that filled Mrs Miller 'with terror and dismay', and the house reached the nadir of its fortunes when it found itself occupied by 'a stout female who kept a certain description of lady lodgers'. On their departure it 'lay untenanted for five years as a result' —

untenanted, that is, with the exception of a ghost. The spectre was reported to be that of a 'murdered gentleman whose throat had been cut in an inner apartment by the ladies and his body flung by night into the deep mud of the harbour'. This representation of events in the former tap-room was reduced to its sad if less spectacular reality when one of the ladies themselves was found by the police 'crouching on a lair of straw' and was promptly 'exorcised' into the Bridewell. That being the last that was seen of the ghost, a tenant was found who was not only willing to occupy the property but to pay the rent as well, a state of affairs much too satisfactory to last. The house, not surprisingly, stood in need of essential and costly repair, and another burden was soon to be added as well in the shape of an increase in the parish rates, the heritors having been 'rated for the erection of the magnificent Parish Church of North Leith then in course of building'.

The year was now 1824 and Hugh Miller, having attained competence 'in the eye of the law' to dispose of his unwanted house, determined to lose no time in seeking 'if not a purchaser, at least some one foolish enough to take it off his hands for nothing'. He was also, opportunities to earn his living in the North being few, eager to search for work 'among the stone cutters of Edinburgh' (then considered the most skilled in their particular craft in the world); so there were two pressing reasons for his presence aboard the Leith smack which, four days after leaving Cromarty, was 'threading her way in a morning of light airs and huge broken fog wreaths' through the Firth of Forth. Soon afterwards 'Leith, with its thicket of masts and its tall round tower' lay before him and he came ashore, a strong, powerfully built, muscular figure whose solemn expression probably belied the sense of humour which, as it frequently reveals itself in the pages of *My Schools and Schoolmasters*, he undoubtedly possessed.

The next day he waited on Mr Veitch, who was able to offer assistance with both undertakings, holding out some hope of a small price for the property and giving him an introduction to a master builder. This was the time of the great building mania in Edinburgh and its environs, and Hugh Miller now found himself, for the ensuing ten months, hewing stones 'under the elm and chestnut trees of Niddrie Park'. A farm servant and his wife in the village took him into their one-roomed cottage, his bed and theirs being on opposite sides with the passage to the door between them. It took him some time to get used to these unaccustomed domestic arrangements. He was even joined, a little later, by a fellow lodger, the goodwife and her husband apparently being in no way put out by such overcrowding and lack of privacy.

This was one of the old eighteenth-century collier villages, now within the boundaries of the City of Edinburgh but then in the country, where the inhabitants had been born into bondage as a consequence of Acts of Parliament which made them the property of the mine owners who employed them, and it took two Acts of Parliament, the second in 1799, to obtain their release from serfdom. Hugh Miller saw it as one of the most singular circumstances of his life that he had conversed with Scotsmen who had been slaves, and the sons of slaves, at the time of their birth only fifty years earlier. Carters and farm labourers made up the rest of the village population and were all, as the stonemason from Cromarty described them, 'ignorant and unintellectual'. Among the colliers, the women bore more marks of serfdom than the men, and theirs had certainly been a hard and soul-destroying life in the pits. They and their children, commonly known as bearers, worked under ground for up to twelve hours a day carrying heavy creels on their backs over long distances from the coal face or, in some mines, ascending ladders till they reached the surface. It was not until 1842 that Lord Shaftesbury with difficulty got a bill through Parliament terminating the engagement of women, and boys under ten years of age, for such employment.

Hugh Miller and his fellow stonemasons were working on additions and improvements at the mansionhouse of Niddrie Marischal, the home of the Wauchopes of Niddrie for eight hundred years. An earlier castle was destroyed in the sixteenth century by an Edinburgh mob because of the 'evil ways' of Archibald Wauchope, the then laird, and although the estate was forfeited and acquired by the Sandilands family, it returned to the Wauchopes in 1608 when the former laird's son made sure of his lost inheritance by marrying a Sandilands daughter. In the seventeenth century John Wauchope of Niddrie was present at the coronation of Charles II, and it was his son who opened new coal workings on his property, paying £54 for sinking a nine-fathom shaft 'at £6 the fathom': £3 went to 'a wife to carrieing the picks too and fra the smiddie' for fifteen days. The price of coal was 2/2d a load. Niddrie Marischal was well known to Lord Cockburn, who wrote in his *Memorials* that he frequently passed Saturdays, Sundays and holidays there for many years.

The last member of this ancient Midlothian family to live in the house was General Andrew Gilbert Wauchope, a compassionate and enlightened man who earned the respect and affectionate loyalty of the Niddrie and New Craighall villagers. He took a keen interest in their welfare, and during the 17-week miners' strike of 1894, when pits were closed throughout the country, he provided his own colliers and their families with food, including vegetables from the Niddrie Marischal garden. The General had been in the Navy during his earlier years and had served with Queen Victoria's son, Prince Alfred, later Duke of Edinburgh. The Prince, when a student at Edinburgh University during the winter of 1863/64 and residing at Holyrood Palace, made several visits to Niddrie where he went pigeon-shooting with his former shipmate. It was General Wauchope's misfortune to have only a brief period of family life. In 1893 he married Jean Muir, daughter of the Principal of the University of Edinburgh, but the war clouds were gathering as the century drew to a close, and he was killed during the Boer War in 1899. Queen Victoria sent a message of sympathy to his widow, who remained at Niddrie Marischal until her death in

1942. The mansionhouse, along with 136 acres of land, was taken over by the Town Council in 1950, and nine years later the house was reduced to an empty shell by a 'spectacular fire', as an Edinburgh newspaper described it at the time. General Wauchope's biographer, William Baird, makes reference to the young stonemason from Cromarty who was employed at Niddrie House in 1824 and who was traditionally believed to have been responsible for the carving of some ornamental chimneys in the mansion.

During his period at Niddrie, Hugh Miller made frequent expeditions to Edinburgh to acquaint himself with the City, climbing Arthur's Seat to watch the sun go down behind the Lomond Hills in Fife, and gaining the same pleasure from the antique aspects of the town as he got from the wild and picturesque countryside with which he was more familiar in the north. He felt that he had seen 'not one, but two cities — a city of the past and a city of the present — set down side by side, as if for purposes of comparison'.

It was not long before he discovered among some of his fellow workmen at Niddrie a predilection for the theatrical entertainments which could be enjoyed in the capital. A seat in the gallery of the Theatre Royal, in Shakespeare Square, cost 1/-, and the stonemasons were usually willing to sacrifice that sum from their wages at the end of the week. Hugh was not as enthusiastic as some of the others, but he made occasional visits to the old theatre in their company. One of them in particular, identified only as 'Davie' and who lodged in another cottage, was a 'wayward, eccentric lad and stage mad'. This rustic devotee of the boards had even written a play himself. Young Miller considered that, for the stage, 'nature had fitted him rather indifferently', it being his misfortune to have 'a squat, ungainly figure, an inexpressive face and a voice that . . . somewhat resembled . . . a carpenter's saw'.

A spectacle of a very different order brought Hugh and his friends hot foot to the City on another occasion. In November 1824 the Great Fire of Edinburgh broke out in the

High Street and Parliament Square and raged unabated for several days. News of the conflagration, in which 400 families were rendered homeless, was soon carried to Niddrie, with the prediction that the masons could now look forward to rebuilding the Old Town in its entirety; so they set off that night to witness the fiery destruction that might give them so much employment in the future.

However restricted and, as he himself considered it until he grew more accustomed to it, unseemly his village lodgings may have been, they were presumably to be preferred to the unsavoury slum in Leith of which he was endeavouring to rid himself, and in order to do so he had to keep company on the occasions when he visited it with a character then notorious in the Port called Peter McCraw who appears to have been as unprepossessing as the property. McCraw was a house agent, a man with only one hand and an unenviable reputation for pitiless persistence in his other capacity, that of tax collector. The place was being used as sleeping quarters by tramps, and a heap of straw in one of the corners indicated the presence of one such unwanted tenant. 'Ah!' said McCraw, 'got in again, I see. The shutters must be looked to.' Other things required looking to as well. The walls were blackened by smoke plaster had fallen, or was still hanging, from the ceiling, and the bars of the grates had rusted till they were as 'red as foxtails'. The stonemason attempted a humorous approach. 'Its terrible to be married for life to a baggage of a house like this and made liable, like other husbands, for all its debts,' he said. 'Is there no way of getting a divorce?' But the house agent was not to be drawn and answered emphatically that he didn't know.

Years afterwards Hugh Miller was surprised to encounter Peter McCraw in a poem, or song, as he expressed it, by 'poor Gilfillan', none other than the Poet of Leith himself, called 'The Tax-Gatherer'. Gilfillan showed little sympathy for his subject in lines that reveal the extent to which McCraw was feared and hated by the local population:

> There's hope o' a ship though she's sair pressed with dangers,
>   An' roun' her frail timmers the angry winds blaw;
> I've aften gat kindness unlooked for frae strangers,
>   But wha need hope kindness frae Peter McCraw?
> I've kent a man pardoned when just at the gallows —
>   I've kent a chiel honest whase trade was the law!
> I've kent fortune's smile even fa' on gude fellows;
>   But I ne'er kent exception wi' Peter McCraw!

The following year Hugh Miller got himself 'as surely dissevered from the Coal-hill as paper and parchment could do it', but the next time he passed 'his umquhile house' it was derelict and boarded up.

After falling a victim to 'stonecutter's malady', caused by the penetration of his lungs by stone dust, he returned to Cromarty where, in the fresh sea air of the North-East coast, the condition improved. He now felt, however, that a change of occupation was essential, not only for the sake of his health but also because his active mind required more intellectual stimulation than could be obtained from the hewing of stones. This led him first to employment in a bank after his marriage to Lydia Fraser, also of Cromarty, but an opportunity to embark on the work for which he was outstandingly suited came in 1839 when he was asked by the Evangelical Party to become the first editor of a newspaper they were about to launch called *The Witness*. This appointment brought him back to Edinburgh, and the family settled at 16 Archibald Place.

The geological articles which were later published collectively under the title of *The Old Red Sandstone* appeared originally in *The Witness*, but he became increasingly interested in, and later obsessively influenced by, the theological controversy which above all others at that time was exercising the minds and consciences of churchmen. The discoveries of Charles Darwin were opening new and disturbing avenues of evolutionary thought, and it was to be many years before Christian thinking would be able to recognise that theology and science were mutually complementary rather than mutually exclusive.

It was in a house called Shrub Mount, beside St. Mark's Church in Portobello, that Hugh Miller spent the last years of his life with his wife and children. Here he created a museum of geology, the study of which, together, later, with theology, had been the principal concern and overriding interest of his life. The adverse effects of mental stress were now becoming apparent in the mind of this 'physical giant', as Sydney Dobell, to whom 'he complained much of his broken health', was to write. He began to have irrational doubts about the safety of his geological collection and even of his own life, and took to sleeping with firearms beside him during the night. In an attempt to answer his critics and to clarify his own fevered thinking on the scientific implications of his discoveries among the fossil-bearing stones that told their own silent but irrefutable story to their investigators, he commenced *The Testimony of the Rocks*, a book destined never to be finished. In 1856, at the age of only 54, he wrote a farewell letter to his wife and put an end to his mental anguish with a revolver.

'His funeral', as James Grant has written, 'was a vast and solemn one.' It was winter, and thawing snow covered the streets, but this did not deter the Edinburgh crowds who came in 'thick masses' to watch in respectful silence the passing of the cavalcade to the Grange Cemetery. Even the shops were closed as the whole town mourned an outstanding Scotsman. Another name in the City's literary galaxy had entered into history, and there was a fine appropriateness in the placing of his grave, for he lies next to Thomas Nelson, one of her greatest publishers.

How many people in the course of a lifetime encounter genius unaware? Among the thick masses in the Portobello streets could there have been some who had hewn stones under the shade of Niddrie Woods some thirty years before? Did the squat, ungainly, stage-struck Davie, or even the callous, one-armed Peter McCraw, if he still survived to wreak injustice in the port of Leith, casting back their minds to see again the stalwart figure of the young stonemason from the Cromarty cottage, salute his memory as he passed on his last untimely journey?

He had paid the price of that rare possession, a mind moulded to pioneer on the edges of human understanding and discovery and, by so doing, had carved out a path for others who were to follow him and, like the rocks themselves, had left his own particular testimony, for there is nothing hidden that shall not ultimately be revealed.

CHAPTER 16

The New Haven

WHILE in the second half of the twentieth century cities expand into sprawling, concrete conurbations and new towns spring up to meet industrial demand in a time of rapid social and scientific change, many of the old centres of maritime trade, commerce and population have subsided into quiet, forgotten backwaters visited only by the painstaking researcher of the past or, where organised publicity has placed them on the tourist tracks, the casual observer and the curious. But this sequence of events is far from being a recent one. It has in fact been taking place, usually on a much more gradual scale, throughout the history of man's relationship with his environment.

An example of this flowing and ebbing tide in the geographical significance of towns and villages is the little hamlet of Blackness on the Firth of Forth. Once the thriving port of the inland town of Linlithgow three miles to the south-west, with its ancient castle guarding the upper reaches of the Forth, it lost its status in proportion as the old trading patterns changed and increased shipping tonnage restricted cargo-carrying vessels to the deeper water of the Forth estuary. It was known as the Haven and when, in 1493, King James IV obtained from Abbot Ballantyne of Holyrood the coastal part of the extensive barony of Broughton for the purpose of dock and harbour building, he saw to it that houses and a rope-walk were provided in addition, and his choice of name for the location of this development was New Haven to distinguish it from the old one. Blackness was a place of some standing at the time when it was customary for Scotland's kings to make frequent use of their Palace at Linlithgow; and when the Regent Moray, during the minority of James VI, was assassinated in the town in 1570, his body was taken to Blackness. From there it was conveyed by sea to

Fig. 36. Newhaven, a fishing village by the Forth in which very few of its
original buildings now survive.

Leith where it lay in the church now known as South Leith
prior to burial within St. Giles in Edinburgh.

The New Haven was also known as Our Lady's Port of
Grace on account of a chapel dedicated to the Virgin there,
fragments of which were still in existence at the end of the
nineteenth century. The chapel was later dedicated to St.
James as well and appears to have been a daughter church of
St. Anthony's Preceptory in Leith, as Grant records that 'in
1614, with its grounds, it was conveyed in the same charter to
the Kirk Session of South Leith by James VI'. As early as 1511
James had granted Newhaven to the Burgesses of Edinburgh,
and the superiority was in fact the first of their voracious

acquisitions which later encompassed nearly the whole of
Leith.

It was here that the famous Forth-built warship, the *Great
Michael*, was constructed by the fourth James, who was
satisfied that in it he possessed the world's finest ocean-going
vessel, which had solid oak amidships as much as ten feet
thick and was launched in 1511, a year no doubt well
remembered by those who witnessed it. But the ship had a
short and undistinguished life. Her instructions, which were
to proceed to France, would seem to have been disobeyed, as
she is next heard of, in the few and rather unreliable surviving
records, as bearing down on the Irish coast in a plundering
raid! After the untimely death of the King at Flodden Field,
the *Michael* was sold to Louis XII, and she was later reported
to have been 'suffered to rot in the harbour of Brest', a sad
end for such a noble craft. James IV did not live to bring his
plans for a Scottish Navy to fruition. It has been said that he
hoped to outstrip the port of Leith with his carefully designed
and up-to-date New Haven, but if so, that popular but
unfortunate monarch was not destined to come within sight
of achieving that ambition either.

As might be expected, Edinburgh owned the Newhaven
oyster fishings and, ceremonial being dear to the heart of all
burgesses, an annual 'stately progress' to the Port was made
for the purpose of assessing the quality and quantity of these
highly marketable delicacies and of 'rouping' the fishings.
They even took to the boats and 'solemnly cruised' above the
oyster beds maturing profitably beneath the Firth. During the
later 1700s the popularity of oysters was at its height, and
high society as well as low spent long hours in the taverns and
oyster cellars of the City where 'raw oysters and flagons of
porter were set out plentifully on a table in a dingy
wainscoted room lighted by tallow candles'. They were in
such demand that the 'home-grown' variety had to be
augmented by others imported frequently from Holland.
Such inroads, in fact, were being made into the oyster
population, and so many seedling oysters taken from the

Fig. 37.   Surviving buildings in Newhaven Village.

water and sold to foreign buyers for the creation of new oyster beds in other countries; that steps were taken to prevent over-dredging. In 1790 an imaginative method of conservation was attempted. Brass and iron 'patterns' were manufactured and distributed to the Newhaven fishermen, specimens being kept in Leith also at the Shore Dues Office; anyone found selling oysters smaller than the size of the pattern was fined and the overseas sale of oysters was banned completely. Beds were also situated at the Black Rocks near Leith Harbour and at Inchkeith, and disputes with Prestonpans over the right to these oyster fishings were not uncommon. Dredging, however, was often carried on under cover of darkness and went undetected. Eventually all efforts to save the oyster scalps of the Forth proved unavailing. In fairness to the Newhaven fishermen it has to be said that the principal damage was done by outsiders who rented the scalps and brought in their own dredging vessels; even the Duke of Buccleuch, who owned some of the oyster beds, was interested only in profit and could not be persuaded to introduce conservation measures. Restocking was contemplated as late as 1897, but long before that the day of the lucrative but abused oyster fishings was at an end.

The old tradition that oysters should only be eaten when there is an R in the month corresponds exactly with the oyster season, which starts at the beginning of September and continues to the end of April. The mussels gathered along the coastline were also a regular source of revenue in the Newhaven Fish Market until as recently as 1955. In that year the shellfish beds were found to be contaminated, and the trade in mussels followed that of the oysters into oblivion.

The Newhaven oyster-women's was one of the best-known and most beautiful of the old street cries of Edinburgh, all now as much a part of history as the traditional costume of the fisherwomen themselves, and their closes and forestaired houses in the village have almost entirely disappeared as well. At the top of the Whale Brae, now part of Newhaven Road, stood Admiralty House (demolished in the 1930s) beside the Fishermen's Park where the nets were set out to dry, and some of the fishing yawls were built in a former sailmaker's shed. The Park was taken over by the City in 1920 and exists no longer. Further up Newhaven Road, and adjoining the Park after which it was called, the much altered, partially Georgian house of Victoria Park still serves the community as a day nursery for children. This house went out of private ownership in 1918 when it was bought by the Town Council of Edinburgh and it was here, during the smallpox epidemic of 1942, that anyone thought liable, through contact with those who suffered from it, to contract the disease was kept in isolation for a period of twenty-one days. After the epidemic the building returned to its former use.

Fig. 38. One of the last remaining closes in Newhaven in 1972.

From the seventeenth century, if not earlier, the services of pilot boats, owned and supervised by a pilot master, were available at Leith and Newhaven where exceptional skill in navigation often bridged the gap between seawreck and survival among the submerged rocks of the Forth in treacherous winter weather. On land, the Newhaven stagecoach, in the early years of the nineteenth century, carried the fishwives and other passengers from the village to the Tron Church and back three times a day, a distance, as the gull flies, of just over two miles.

During the middle years of the nineteenth century the regular loading of gunpowder on to Government ships at

Newhaven was, not surprisingly, a source of concern to the residents of the village itself and of neighbouring Trinity. The danger was greatly increased by the casual behaviour of the seamen handling the lethal barrels, who smoked their pipes, in spite of fines and reprimands, while so employed. As happens in any age when adverse local opinion has been roused, a public meeting was held to consider what should be done, and an appeal was immediately sent to the Home Secretary in London. The appeal proved effective, and in 1874 the shipment of gunpowder was removed to Leith.

In the Peacock Hotel, always famed for its fish, Newhaven has had for many years a picturesque link with its past both architecturally and gastronomically. Peacock was the name of the original owner, and in a recent restoration an old fireplace decorated with a well-preserved peacock in coloured tiles was discovered, as well as a group of three stained-glass windows which had been boarded up. Another building, the Newhaven Free Fishermen's Hall built in 1877, was reconstructed a few years ago along with adjoining property to form new premises for a motor boat club, the interior being remodelled to resemble that of King James IV's Newhaven-built warship, the *Great Michael*.

The men of Newhaven have been noted for their courage both in peace and war. In January 1816 a Scandinavian vessel, in danger of foundering off Inchkeith, flew a distress signal from her masthead which was sighted by the Newhaven pilots. Nine of them set out to the rescue in heavy seas about ten o'clock in the morning and succeeded by strenuous effort in getting three men on board. They were only just in time, as the master was ordering the masts to be cut down. Thanks to their expert seamanship and local knowledge the narrow waters between rocks to the south of the island were safely negotiated, and the vessel was able to reach the shelter of Elie harbour without misadventure, the captain gratefully paying the one hundred guineas charged by the Newhaven pilots whose lives had been in danger throughout. At the beginning of the nineteenth century the fee was £3:3/- for normal pilotage from the May Island into Leith roads for ships of 150 tons and over, but only £2:12:6 if the vessel was 'two leagues above the May'.

The fishermen of Newhaven won praise for their conspicuous patriotism during the war with France, when they formed themselves into a marine defence force to guard the coastline. In recognition of this service a silver medal was presented to the Newhaven Free Fishermen's Society in 1796 and was worn by the Society's boxmaster every year during their procession through Leith, Edinburgh, Granton and Trinity. Unfortunately a letter signed by George III 'expressing his satisfaction at their loyalty' was lost after being preserved by the Society for many years.

During the 1860s the Town Council of Leith would appear to have been experiencing difficulty in keeping the streets of Newhaven in good order, as a number of prosecutions are recorded in the *Leith Burghs Pilot*. These consisted principally of the throwing of rubbish in the shape of cabbage leaves and potato peelings on to the roads and pavements, and for this offence a fine of about half a crown with the option of four days' imprisonment was usually imposed. Some boys, who would persist in being boys, were severely warned and admonished for stealing apples and causing damage to private gardens, and then dismissed, in 1864. The commonest offences were drunkenness and disorderly behaviour and the stealing of coal, but in 1881 two women were jailed for ten days after taking three cotton sheets and a linen apron from a clothes line on the public thoroughfare in Darling's Close in Leith — a nineteenth-century version of shoplifting! Petty crimes and the names of their perpetrators were the stuff of local news reporting, along with verbatim reports of deliberations in the Leith Town Council Chamber, and a surprising and comprehensive coverage of foreign news. Devoid, of course, of photographs, but presenting column after extensive column of well-printed, well-written and, in accordance with the higher if more pedantic literary standards of the time, meticulously expressed information on current

Fig. 39. Newhaven Harbour and Lighthouse, once the colourful scene of the still famous fishwives in their traditional costume.

affairs and prevailing public opinion, the *Leith Burghs Pilot* circulated through Leith, Portobello, Dalkeith, Newhaven, Granton and Cramond and was beyond doubt excellent value at one old penny. An editorial note in one edition is indicative of the manners that maketh man in any period of history but would never, like so much else, find a place among present-day journalese: 'We shall be willing at all times to throw our columns open to correspondents who write in a gentlemanly and courteous spirit, whatever their views might be; and shall give correspondents of diametrically opposite opinions an impartial hearing'.

Of the old historic fishing village, there is not much to be encountered on the ground today. Late twentieth-century housing casting a few backward glances at tradition cannot perpetuate the distinctive personality of the original New

Haven and, unlike its predecessor Blackness, there is no ancient fortress around which to concentrate an imaginative recreation of its significant years. To attempt this, the harbour is probably the most promising place, with its colourful fleet of little boats and the white lighthouse on the seawall lifting its eye unto the Firth. The creels and petticoats of the fisher lassies are to be seen there no more and, like the oysters and the inimitable street cries of their vendors, are not likely to return.

CHAPTER 17

History from an Early Newspaper

THE date is Saturday, February 28th 1807, two years after Trafalgar and eight years before Waterloo in the reign of George III; the title *The Caledonian Mercury*; the printer Robert Allan at the Old Fishmarket Close in Edinburgh; and the price sixpence.

The reason for the survival for nearly two hundred years of a four-page, closely printed newspaper, in which references to Leith are numerous, in the family of the original owner is not now known, but a keen interest in (and an awarenes of the historic nature of the outcome of) the bitter controversy then occupying the minds and printing presses of the period surrounding the brutal and all too financially profitable slave trade is certainly a possible explanation. It was in that eventful year of 1807 that Britain finally abolished that barbaric practice in its colonial empire, and under the proud heading of 'Imperial Parliament' the last passionate debate in the House of Commons, and the passing of the Bill by an overwhelming majority, can still be deciphered in the minutely printed columns of this brittle, faded forerunner of the mass media, where it is presented as it took place without comment or criticism; and also without illustration, as photography was still as unknown as wireless or the internal combustion engine.

After so momentous an event the daily mundanities of the time seem anti-climactic by comparison, but are also of interest in their own right as a microcosm of local social history at the beginning of a century which, as we move towards the year 2000, is becoming increasingly remote.

The intermittent Napoleonic Wars were in progress and, Leith not yet having been superseded by the Clyde as Scotland's most important arrival and departure point for merchant shipping, there are several announcements of loading dates for vessels 'armed by Government' against enemy interception on the high seas. 'At Leith for London', reads one such advertisement, 'The Old Shipping Co.'s Smack Caledonia, Robt. Nisbet Master, will take goods till Tuesday morning at nine o'clock.' 'The John is a new vessel, about 300 tons burden, and sails fast', says another, with the information that she will leave for Halifax and Prince Edward Island on 20th March. Also 'at Leith taking in goods for London direct' is the 'Union Shipping Company's Smack, armed with six 18-pound carronades, Eliza, Mark Sanderson Master', which will sail on Tuesday morning at 8 o'clock. The Sloop *Hope* was anchored at Leith as well, waiting to receive goods on board for Shetland, and would sail on 6th March.

Victuallers and provision merchants advertise their wares without recourse to sales promotion tricks or stratagems. James Reid of the Luckenbooths can supply his customers with 'new Pickled Herrings, of an excellent quality, just arrived from the West Highlands in Barrels, Firkins and Half Firkins' along with 'Aberdeen pickled cod in Small Kitts for the convenience of private families', as well as 'Virgin Honey in Jars of one and two pints each'. 'Tickets for a Lottery' makes surprising reading. These could be obtained at the Licensed Office of Dan Forrest opposite the Tron Church. In the two preceding Lotteries capital prizes of £20,000 and £500 had been sold in shares, which would seem to indicate that gambling was as popular and profitable in the Edinburgh of the early nineteenth century as honey and salted fish.

The timber trade was also flourishing and, imported from the Baltic, wood destined for panelling and furniture had been unloaded regularly on the quays at Leith for at least two hundred years. 'To be peremptorily sold at auction', states one announcement succinctly, 'in Martin's Coal Yard, Constitution Street, Leith, on Mon. 2 March at 12 o'clock, 700 Christiana Red Wood Deals 10–12 feet in length . . . and 300 Gottenburg Deals.' A police force was in the early stages of its development in the Port, and an advertisement for a suitable person to take charge was inserted with a commendable economy of words: 'Wanted for the towns of

South and North Leith, Citadel, Coal Hill, Territory of St. Anthony and Yardheads an Intendent of Police'. And another item not likely to be read in any newspaper of the present day concerned 'deserters from His Majesty's 43 (or Argyllshire) Regiment of British Militia' and listed eleven names with detailed descriptions of the men involved.

In spite of war and rumours of invasion, social activities continued without interruption, and the paper gives due space to the current entertainments.

The sixth and last subscription concert of the season at Corrie's Rooms was to be followed, as usual, by a Grand Ball — 'admission to non-subscribers 5/-'. Mr N. Corrie is listed in the Edinburgh Post Office Directory for 1807 as a music seller with Concert Rooms in Leith Walk. He begged leave 'to return his warmest thanks to the subscribers for the present season, and to express his hopes that they intend continuing their subscriptions' for the next, for which subscription books 'were now open at Mr Corrie's music shop'. And if these pleasurable distractions were not enough to raise the spectators' spirits and banish their fears, they could always have recourse to Dr Innes' Compound Strengthening Powders, obtainable in sealed parcels, price 6/- including duty, from 'Mr Manderson, apothecary, in Rose Street'. Their salutary effects in restoring 'the weak, debilitated and nervous constitutions of the young and old of both sexes to health and vigour', while not guaranteed, were clearly considered to be beyond reasonable dispute.

Another announcement concerning Leith is interesting in that it reflects the longstanding antagonism between the City and its Port: 'A notice having appeared in this paper, addressed to the inhabitants of Leith, calculated to induce a belief that the Magistrates and Council of this city had relinquished altogether a plan they have in view for certain improvements at the west end of Leith Links, we are authorised to state that this is by no means the case, and that the plan has been given up for the present, not in consequence of any intimation, as erroneously stated in the anonymous notice, but with a view of accelerating the passing of an Act of Parliament, the leading purposes of which are totally different and unconnected with Leith Links, of which the Magistrates and Council, as representing the community of Edinburgh, are proprietors'.

The advertisements dealing with property for sale and to let are presented in a picturesque linguistic style: 'That house in Clamshell Turnpike entering from the High Street' (Edinburgh — Old Town) 'which may, at a trifling expense, be converted into two', can be seen 'every lawful day from 1 to 3'. By order of the Lord Provost and Magistrates several building lots are offered for sale — the remaining areas, on the west and east ends of London Street on the north side, and one or two gap sites as yet unbuilt on in Charlotte Square together with stable ground behind (Edinburgh — New Town which in 1807 was still in course of building). A house in Nicolson Street 'lately possessed by the Honourable Miss Grey, above Mr Core's china shop' is to be rouped on the 6th of March. 'Three sides of a square, to be called Hermitage Square, measuring upwards of six acres English, part of the lands of Hermitage' are to be feued for building. This desirable residential site is 'within five minutes' walk of Leith, and ten minutes' walk of the sea-beach, where machines for bathing can be had at all hours'. It might well be wondered whether the opportunity for a midnight dip would be attractive to potential buyers on the east-windswept east coast, but its convenient situation for recreations more suited to the climate might have been considered favourable. Bounded on the north by the lands belonging to Lady Fife, the ground commanded a most extensive view of the Firth of Forth, the City of Edinburgh, the town of Leith and the adjacent country, and lay 'two or three hundred yards from the Golf-house of Leith, entering by the road from Leith to Lochend'.

No. 3 St. James's Place, Leith, 'being in a pleasant, healthy situation' on the north side of the road leading to Jock's Lodge, is on offer, along with the large and commodious house called Bonnington Lodge 'situate on the road to Newhaven' with a hay-loft and stable with two stalls suitable for 'a large and genteel family'. Details of extensive accommodation are given for several of the houses in this section, including such features — unlikely to sharpen their competitive selling edge for future generations — as garrets, closets, coal- and wash-houses, cellars, catacombs (as those cold and dark old dungeons with recesses or pigeon-holes for the storage of wine were called) and water-pumps which were needed to get the water, now available by dint of primitive plumbing in individual houses, above the level of the basement.

The notice that 'On Wednesday the 2nd batallion of the 42nd regiment, or Royal Highlanders, marched through this city for Leith, where they are to embark for Fort George', brings us back to the War and the coastline defences against a possible French invasion; and the reported death of Mr William Simpson, a papermaker at Lasswade, takes us back to a still earlier war in the reign of George III, as Mr Simpson 'had served under Lord Cornwallis, as an officer of artillery, during the American War'.

It is doubtful if newspapers of the late twentieth century, even allowing for photographs, banner headlines and two-page-spread advertisements, offer their readers more balanced, impartial, varied and well-presented news in the much greater space at their disposal than is contained in the four faded and fascinating pages of this once-folded single sheet. Every effort had been made to include the latest and most accurate reports, without benefit of telephone or radio, from the theatres of war, and the account of Parliamentary proceedings is ingrained with the natural assumption that Great Britain deserved its name and would never lose its greatness or its power. The triumph of terminating the odious traffic in human lives was all the greater for having been accomplished by a nation at war and, as G.M. Trevelyan was to write over a century later, 'If Wilberforce could convert England, she would soon persuade the world'. And in 1807 that was exactly what she did.

CHAPTER 18

Houses by the Forth

THERE are many reasons why people put down roots, but in bygone times they tended to be closely linked with the potential of particular areas to provide the basic environmental requirements for survival and their possible subsequent development for future prosperity. It was in such favourable places that families became established, sometimes for generation after generation, passing on what they had achieved to be built on and expanded by their successors, and it is this process of land selection that explains the numbers of old and interesting houses in distinctive groupings in different parts of the country. Fertile soil for food production and coastal belts and natural harbours for fishing and trading are natural locations in which a rich heritage of vernacular tradition and its attendant architecture are principally to be found. In varying degrees all these features were there for the exploiting around the shores of Forth, and it is therefore not surprising that such houses as have fortunately survived, in whole or in part, to the present day should be full of local, and sometimes national, history and general interest.

Furthest to the east, and situated at the edge of the coalmining district that stretches across to Musselburgh, is Brunstane House, approached across a bridge which is itself of interest because of age but, dating in fact from the eighteenth century, is not as old as tradition, which harks it back to the Romans, would suggest. Originally known as Gilbertoun, the house belonged in the early years of the sixteenth century to John Crichton, who gave it the name of Brunstane after his castle near Penicuik. Alexander Crichton, his son, was involved in the murder of Cardinal Beaton, and the building was pulled down in consequence. John Geddie describes how, in 1593, the lands were alienated to 'Dame Jane Fleming, Lady Thirlestane, the widow of Chancellor

Fig. 40.   Brunstane House, the Edinburgh home of the notorious Earl of Lauderdale during the reign of Charles II.

Maitland', and her son, the first Earl of Lauderdale, entered into possession of them. His more famous son, John Maitland, afterwards Duke of Lauderdale, succeeded to them, and his arms, together with those of his first wife, were carved over the entrance, beside the date 1639, when he had completed the rebuilding of the mansion. About thirty years later the Duke, strong, unscrupulous, a member of the notorious Cabal of Charles II, and a mighty wielder of unopposed power in Scotland, greatly strengthened the historic interest of Brunstane by employing the King's Architect in Scotland, Sir William Bruce, to enlarge the house. The Duchess having died in January 1671, Lauderdale embarked upon his second marriage the following month to the probably disreputable and certainly scheming and determined Countess of Dysart. She was also the cousin of her new husband's architect, and it is worth noting that Sir William Bruce's second wife spent her widowhood in the demilitarised Citadel in Leith after his death.

Brunstane House was enlarged by Bruce in much the same way as he extended Holyrood Palace for Charles II. A projecting corner tower was built to correspond with the older tower already in existence, and both structures were then linked by a symmetrical central range containing the entrance. Perhaps the most interesting apartment in the house is the octagonal dining-room, 'wainscotted and ceilinged', says John Geddie, 'in dark oak, with elaborately ornamented chimneypiece, bearing the royal and the Lauderdale arms, and with panel-paintings (of which there are over seventy in the house) — the scene of much wassailing and of good, or more often evil, counselling in the most troubled time in the history of the Scottish Church and State'. The building contains some of the earliest sash windows in the country.

After the Lauderdales, Brunstane passed to the Duke of Argyle and in 1747 together with part of the estate, to Andrew Fletcher of Saltoun, Lord Justice-Clerk at the time of the '45, who died there in 1766. Three years later it was bought by the eighth Earl of Abercorn, who already owned the remaining lands through their having been purchased by the third Earl from the Duke of Argyle, and he in turn sold the house to the Benhar Coal Company in 1875. With extensive alterations by William Adam and plasterwork of exceptional merit, the house, which is still in occupation, retains much of its former splendour and is a building of both local and national importance.

Brunstane stands well back from the sea, behind the streets of Joppa and the Brunstane Burn that runs beneath the 'Roman' bridge, and the attractively composed walls and turrets of Craigentinny House are also some distance from the water. In the old vernacular style with extensions of the seventeenth and nineteenth centuries, it was the home of the Nisbets of Dean and Craigentinny and, latterly, of the Millers, a merchant family whose eldest sons were always called William. The house and surrounding lands were acquired by William Miller, a Quaker seed merchant from Holyrood Road, when the Nisbets died out in 1764. John Russell calls the house the most interesting of the mansions of Restalrig. In 1780, so tradition has it, the laird, being in his 91st year, considered the time had come to ensure the succession to yet another of his name, and installed in his house a bride said to be rather less than forty years his junior. The idea of settling down immediately did not apparently appeal, and they embarked on an odyssey of European travel. When news reached his tenants that another William had been born in Paris — his mother being in fact 42 — they inclined towards a degree of scepticism, but the nonagenarian parent and his wife returned, and the child was brought up at Craigentinny where in due course he inherited the estate.

Not surprisingly, the last of the William Millers, though becoming a public figure and Member of Parliament for an English constituency, was an eccentric character, not the least of his oddities being the instructions contained in his will, presumably intended to discourage the curious from digging up his remains to discover the secret of his peculiarities. The directions were observed to the letter when he was buried on his own estate, a short distance from the Portobello Road, beneath forty feet of earth and with a large, elaborate monument on top. Known as the Craigentinny Marbles and completed in 1866, the Monument caused widespread interest at the time and can still be seen among the surrounding streets and beyond the grey stone walls of the old farmhouse of Wheatfield. Built in the style of a diminutive Greek temple, it replicates a tomb on the Appian Way in Rome and was designed by the Edinburgh architect, David Rhind. The sculptured panels depicting the overthrow of Pharaoh in the Red Sea and the Song of Miriam and Moses were the work of Alfred Gatley.

Fig. 41.   The Craigentinny Marbles; a diminutive Greek temple, it marks the grave of the eccentric William Miller beside the Portobello Road.

There have been other houses of distinction in this area, and one which has survived among the modern complexities of Leith housing developments and has in recent years been rediscovered is the Regency villa at Seafield called Seacote House. It is now a B-listed building and dates from around 1820 but stands in need of some attention and repair. About three years ago a plan was agreed to convert it into two flats, with the grounds providing space for new houses within a landscaped development project, possibly on similar lines to those carried out at Easter Park, an interesting 'reproduction' house at Barnton, and also overlooking the sea across a golf course, built in the Adam manner in 1905 by a family well

Fig. 42. Drylaw House, a beautiful 18th century mansion now redeveloped to meet 20th century requirements.

known in the tea trade called Melrose and last owned by the Younger family who sold it with its grounds to a developer. In the Autumn of 1983, however, events took a different turn when a construction company applied for permission to demolish Seacote and build six dwellinghouses on the site. This application was fortunately unsuccessful, and it is to be hoped that at least the original decision to retain the villa and create a new residential enclave around it will be allowed to proceed.

Drylaw, another historic house away to the west, is also well distanced from the Firth. Unseen from outside, it hides among green lawns and fruit trees and behind old weathered walls and was originally built in 1707. Like many others, this early Georgian dwelling was turned back to front when reconstructed in 1735, and the short flight of steps with curving iron rails at the back marks the former entrance. The new ashlar facade added at the later date to the other side displays all the distinguishing features — columned portico, astragals, segmental fanlight and central pediment — of the new and developing style. Inside are small pine-panelled rooms and a brass-finialed, wrought-iron staircase recalling the slightly earlier one, mentioned later, at Caroline Park. Too late to be a Bruce house and too early even for William Adam, famous father of more famous sons, its original rubble walls and harling, its layout and conception generally make Drylaw a typical and wholly satisfying Scottish house of its period and an exemplary manifestation of indigenous culture absorbing and subsuming outside influences to create a recognisable national idiom. Although it is known that the Loch family, who built the house, were on terms of personal friendship with the Adams, there is no documentary evidence to support the suggestion that they were involved in designing it. Redevelopment has recently overtaken both house and grounds. Nearby the original Drylaw Mains farmhouse does duty as a police station on the Ferry Road.

Not far from the Firth and, like Brunstane, at one time belonging to the ducal family of Argyle, Caroline Park was built by Viscount Tarbat about 1685, with an ironwork balcony above a projecting portico between two towers. The chief ornaments of the interior are the magnificent staircase with wrought-iron leaves and scrolls of great vigour and beauty, and painted panels on the walls and ceilings. The house came into the possession of the Dukes of Buccleuch from those of Argyle by marriage. The eldest daughter of John, known as 'the celebrated Duke of Argyle' in the eighteenth century, was called Caroline as her mother had been a maid of honour to Queen Caroline, the wife of George II, and the house was so named, it is presumed, after both of them. It has been its misfortune to find itself in industrialised

Fig. 43. The mansionhouse of Caroline Park, an imposing ducal residence in a deteriorated environment.

surroundings in recent times, flanked on the west by a gasworks and by an oil depot on the east. Close at hand, and once a more seemly neighbour to this noble seventeenth-century mansion, are the last fragments of the old ruins of Granton Castle which was probably built, say MacGibbon and Ross, after Hertford's invasion in 1544.

The grounds of Granton House, to the east of the present-day West Shore Road, have been completely swallowed up by the massive Scottish Gas complex on this extensive site. The house was a classical building, three storeys high, with a balustraded roof, and contained twenty-four rooms, including a panelled dining-room. For about twenty years it was the home of Sir John McNeill of Colonsay who died in 1883. Among his guests was Florence Nightingale, who stayed at the house on several occasions. Lord Gifford, the Scottish judge who inaugurated the Gifford Lectures on Religion and died in 1887, also lived here.

Unoccupied and likely to remain so by 1946, the mansion was taken over by Edinburgh Corporation who used it as emergency accommodation, and in 1953 twelve families had found refuge there. Unhappily, on 1st January the following year Granton House was almost completely gutted by fire, after which all hope of rebuilding it was abandoned.

The fate of Granton House is an all too familiar story, but a much stranger one can be told of a little dwelling of very different character in Granton. During the mid-1830s, when the Duke of Buccleuch was building Granton Harbour, the stone for its construction was brought from a quarry which had been opened a mile or more to the west at Granton Point beyond Granton Castle and Caroline Park. The quarry aroused widespread interest when a great fossil tree — an Araucaria 75 feet long — was discovered and had to be left *in situ* as it was too large and heavy to be taken to a museum. The overseer, Mr Robert Muir, lived in a house on the edge of the quarry with a powerful pumping engine in the basement which kept down the water level, and a little garden which he took great pride in cultivating. Twenty years later, as more and more stone was being won from the quarry, fears were expressed about its safety, and the men were given permission to work on the landward faces only. But anxieties were reinforced by a season of severe storms and winds. Confidence being restored, however, as the weather improved, the quarrymen slept soundly in their beds again — all except Mr Muir who awoke suddenly one night with a feeling of unease although no wind was blowing and no alarming sounds were to be heard. Looking up from his bed, he noticed a large crack in the ceiling above his head. As he watched the crack grew steadily wider and wider and, with only a few seconds to spare, he roused his family and quickly hustled them outside. At the same moment the sea rushed in from the submerging quarry and half of the house disappeared beneath the water. When the men arrived for work in the morning, all they could see were planks of wood, wheelbarrows and bits of furniture floating in the Firth. Attempts were made to recover some valuable equipment from the water, but the cost proved to be too great and they were abandoned. After this near disaster, the first marine station for scientific research in Great Britain was built on the site at Granton Point some years afterwards and was opened on 15th April 1884. Besides a floating laboratory, it also had a steam yacht used for dredging and taking soundings.

On high ground overlooking Granton Harbour Lufra House, formerly Lufra Cottage, is now approached from the sea side, and its original gate and entranceway are closed. It was occupied by a shipping agent in 1860.

On the opposite side of West Shore Road from Granton House the Georgian, castellated, B-listed mansion of Craigroyston can be seen beyond its surrounding trees and lawns, and it also is now in the ownership of Scottish Gas. Built about 1800, its rooftop battlements resemble two square tower heads, and it has an arched doorway in its Gothic porch. The bay windows were inserted later, and additions and considerable internal alterations were made by Sir Robert Lorimer in 1907–8. Craigroyston was in use as a Naval Headquarters during the War.

In 1776 William Davidson, having in the best tradition of Scottish merchants spent many years trading in Rotterdam, amassing by his industry sufficient wealth to purchase an estate, acquired the barony of Muirhouse close to the shore above the Cramond Esplanade. The original house built here for himself and his family was replaced in 1832 by the present conspicuous mansion in Marine Parade, still known as Muirhouse. A square tower rises above this asymmetrical, two-storeyed, ecclesiastically-windowed Tudor pile with chimneys like tall pinnacles, and interesting features of the

Fig. 44. Muirhouse, a conspicuous seaside mansion built by the Davidsons of Davidson's Mains in 1832.

interior are the frescoes painted by Zephaniah Bell in the drawing-room when the house was rebuilt in 1832. Muirhouse is an A-listed building and has served as office premises for commercial enterprise in recent years.

The founding family gave its name to Davidson's Mains, and it was from them that Randall Thomas Davidson, Chaplain to Queen Victoria in 1878 and Archbishop of Canterbury from 1903 to 1928, was descended. As Archbishop of Canterbury he crowned King George V in 1911. On the other side of the road the former Muirhouse Mains is now a caravan site, but an altered farm building remains as a substantial relic of its rural past.

A short distance to the west, the Victorian house once known as Broomfield overlooks the water and its stone-strewn shoreline beyond trees and the grass banks on which it stands. Built in the mid-nineteenth century, it belonged to an aunt of the same Earl Haig who gave his name to the First World War Ex-Servicemen's Settlement in Trinity. Broomfield was suggested as a suitable clubhouse for a golf course which was under consideration in 1938, but the whole scheme was abandoned and the course was never laid out. The grey stone house, with its prominent chimneys and many gables, is now better known as the Commodore Hotel and has a large modern extension to the east.

Since the early years when the first developers sank their taproots in the virgin soil of the coastal belt, and farmed and fished and traded and raised substantial houses for themselves and their descendants, later and more numerous roots have been put down as well, and serried rows of suburban dwellings have spread across the Wardie Muir, their numbers increasing with the present-day rapid rise in flat and villa building. To conserve the ancient places beside the new is to ensure a continuity of history — a history in stone — a heritage of houses.

Index